Send in the Idiots

Stories from the
Other Side of Autism

KAMRAN NAZEER

BLOOMSBURY

First published in Great Britain 2006
This paperback edition published 2007

Copyright © 2006 by Kamran Nazeer

The moral right of the author has been asserted

Bloomsbury Publishing Plc, 36 Soho Square, London W1D 3QY

ISBN 97807475 8565 7

10 9 8 7 6 5 4 3 2 1

Typeset by Hewer Text UK Ltd, Edinburgh
Printed in Great Britain by Clays Limited, St Ives plc

www.bloomsbury.com/kamrannazeer

All papers used by Bloomsbury Publishing are natural,
recyclable products made from wood grown in well-managed
forests. The manufacturing processes conform to the
environmental regulations of the country of origin.

Introduction

MS. RUSSELL STOPPED READING newspapers in 1982. She was never the sort of person who read the paper over breakfast. She had incredible difficulties with depth perception which didn't ease until an hour after she woke. In carrying out simple tasks like turning on the shower or doing up buttons, she relied on touch and memory. She avoided buying clothes with small buttons – she remembers a beautiful green dress in particular that she had to turn down (if only it had a zip) – and cooking breakfast, even making toast, bore the prospect of self-harm. It didn't help that there was no breakfast to read her paper over; though, in any case, at that time in the morning, each word appeared on a different plane with the headlines in columns two and four forming a pattern like a crossword puzzle in mid-air.

On the way out of her building – a brownstone terraced house on the Upper West Side of Manhattan – she asked Mrs. Wilson, a neighbor who liked to sit on the stairs leading down from the door, to check that she hadn't missed any buttons or put foundation in her hair by mistake. By that time, her vision had begun to settle. She sat on the steps for ten minutes or so, talking to Mrs. Wilson about television programs or folk singers, and then the streets were even enough for her to walk to work.

She bought a newspaper every morning, from a vendor who stared at her breasts when making change, on the street corner before the school in which she worked. She was a teacher and there was always something to do when she arrived, a parent who needed talking to or an activity that needed setting up. The first class started at 9.30 a.m. and ran through till 11. But none of this – being unable to use the natural lull between getting dressed and going to work in which to read quietly on her own; the rote low-level harassment from the guy in the news stall who kept a cigarette behind his ear, though she never saw him smoke; having to wait till 11 by which time, she often felt, the news had changed – was the reason why she stopped reading newspapers. The reason why Ms. Russell stopped reading newspapers in 1982 was Craig.

Ms. Russell taught a class of autistic children. The students were nursery age. Some of them didn't speak. Some of them didn't take their parents' hands to cross the street on their way to school. One of them insisted on sitting on the white stripe in the multicolored rug in her classroom and would not sit anywhere else. It was the only class in one of the only schools in New York that had designed a special program for autistic children. Even that school had been founded re- cently and with private benefactions. When Ms. Russell was interviewed for her job, the building was still being refur- bished. The walls in the interview room, which became the director's office, were unpainted and there was no desk for the panel to sit behind. At the time, one organization working with autistic children estimated that autism was going undiagnosed in seventy-five per cent of cases; the first significant pieces of research were just beginning; *Rain Man* – the film for which Dustin Hoffman, starring as an autistic person, went on to win an Oscar – hadn't been made yet. Public awareness of the condition was low, the level of medical attention only a little higher.

The school's first students mostly came from affluent backgrounds. They had already been to the few specialists in autism; their parents could afford the high fees for those consultations and for enrolment in the school. The school received regular visits from university researchers and administrators from other schools. The director sometimes asked her staff to imagine that the school existed in a Petri dish and they should assume that everything they did would be observed for its effects.

Ms. Russell was part of the core group of three teachers. It was only after the first class of the morning, when the children were having their 11 a.m. snack, that she got an opportunity to read her newspaper. She sat in one of the bay windows, with a glass of milk, as one of the other teachers supervised the break. The ritual began one morning when one of the students, a six-year-old named Elizabeth, asked her to read the newspaper aloud. As soon as Ms. Russell started to do so, the others shifted their attention too. They listened carefully that first time, and continued to do so, and she enjoyed doing it. So it became a fixture, almost a formal class activity. Their reactions to the reading started going into the reports written by the school's psychologists.

It was at that point that Craig started demonstrating

echolalia. Echolalia, or the constant, disconnected use of a particular word or phrase, is one example of rhythmic or repetitive behaviour, a trait common among autistic people. This is also often described as the desire for local coherence, the preference that autistic people frequently demonstrate for a limited, though immediate, form of order as protection against complexity or confusion. An autistic child will remain entirely unaffected by another person's anger or happiness, of an argument going on between its parents ten meters away, so long as that child is allowed to ensure that all its toy cars are perfectly lined up along the skirting board. Even many autistic adults deal with discomfiting events by returning to a regime – it may be as simple as rocking, or it may involve multiplying three-digit prime numbers. One clinician provides a list of 'coherentizing behaviours' that includes: whirling on own initiative; whirling when given a turn of the head; running to and fro; bouncing; walking on toes and in other peculiar ways; banging or rolling heads; mouthing and licking things; grinding teeth; blinking; moving fingers as if double-jointed or made of dough; and sitting or standing in one place for hours.

More easily, these are quirks, and they are what many people expect autistic individuals to exhibit – small, obsessive activities that provide some sort of enclosure from the world. This is not an unreasonable description. Autistic people *are* confined, to a greater or lesser extent, to a world of their own. The term 'autism' arrives, by a fairly short route, from the Greek *autos*, meaning 'self'.

During Ms. Russell's readings, Craig's echolalia became focussed on the term 'Send in the Idiots'. No one could work out where he got it from and no one could stop him from using it.

'Gridlock continues between the White House and Congress . . .'

'Send in the Idiots.'

'Firefighters prepare for a third day of attempting to contain the blazing forest fires in southern California . . .'

'Wait, miss.'

'Yes, Craig?'

'Send in the Idiots.'

The Idiots were never deployed but Ms. Russell finally accepted defeat. There was no room left in her day for reading the newspaper. The one moment she had found was ruined by a child who wouldn't understand why she was telling him off. So she never did. She just stopped reading aloud. And the children wouldn't let her read on her own. Then she stopped entirely.

Craig left the school the following year. His parents decided to return him to the mainstream education system. He went to a Jesuit school just as his father had done. His father taught him a few lines from the work of Saint Thomas Aquinas, which proved to be a bad move, for Craig started repeating those lines incessantly, and though this impressed the priests initially, it soon led to him regularly being sent to the corner of the classroom and told to face the wall. He infuriated the Brothers further by running his fingers up and down or across the angle that the walls made as they met. On one occasion, he explained patiently to the headmaster that, by his reckoning, the walls definitely weren't perpendicular and that the building may have structural problems.

Nowadays, from time to time, Craig is quoted in newspapers. The words are never attributed to him but he recognizes them and people in the same profession do too. Craig is a speech-writer, working mostly for the Democratic party. Elizabeth, who first asked Ms. Russell to start reading the newspaper to the class, committed suicide in 2002. There was also André. And Randall. And at least a dozen others. I was the child who insisted on sitting on the white stripe in the rug. We don't remember each other very well. Randall feels that thinking back to his time in the school is like looking through a flip-book. Except, as the pages turn, the child in the picture changes into someone else, and then someone else again, and he cannot fix on the names of any of them, or whether they are the child that he saw in the park three days ago cautiously approaching a duck, or one of the children from the school.

In this book, I will tell the stories of the four that I have mentioned, of how they have emerged into adulthood. Before I started writing, with the exception of Craig, I hadn't seen them in twenty years. Even Craig I had met only once, in the summer before college, and we barely spoke to one another, resisting our parents' desire that we bond instantaneously. Finding my classmates was going to be straightforward – our parents had each other's details – but I didn't know whether they'd agree to be in this book. I had the pitch prepared that I would change names and other details, insulate their lives, but it might not work. I didn't know how they thought about their condition. It might be a source of strength: 'I have overcome this.' Though they might not have overcome it and it might equally be an unsaid thing, like the drowning accident in which a childhood friend perished, that you only think about when you have to get on a boat but you're then not able to bypass the memory; you shiver, you make some excuse and stay behind.

I will also tell the story of Ms. Russell – I can call her Rebecca, now that I am an adult too – who still works with autistic children, and has begun to read weekly news magazines from time to time, though never newspapers.

There are certain things that are missing from the lives of autistic individuals. Craig, for example, couldn't tell that Rebecca enjoyed reading the newspaper aloud and that he spoiled it for her. Autistic individuals find it difficult to develop intuition or empathy. In meeting my classmates again and writing about their lives, I want to understand how a life is different when it lacks these elements or when they're not fully formed. So much of what animates our lives – conversation, thought, creativity, friendship, politics – draws on understanding the world of other people and yet autistic people may only be able to rely on one *autos*, their own. By finally sending in the Idiots, as Craig so often suggested, I hope to see more clearly not only the substance of their lives but the nature of the world that lies beyond their reach.

1

'YOU TALK, I TALK, you talk,' suggested André's sister, Amanda, as we watched André walk off fiercely, leaning forward as if into a gale, his hands already withdrawn into the sleeves of his sweatshirt. I was making a mess of both sitting and standing, not knowing whether to go after him or to stay. I eventually gave my bag a gentle kick and dropped back into my seat. I had yet to clear security and André had taken my boarding card. 'He'll need a few minutes,' added Amanda. He was gone from view.

I had spent three straight days living with André in Boston and this had happened six times. I was annoyed at my indiscipline and my inability to anticipate his outrage. On the second occasion, two glasses had been flung against a wall. On the third, he had locked me in the bathroom. After that, I stopped trying to apologize immediately after it happened. That simply made it worse.

I didn't remember him having a temper. When I thought back to André at our school in New York, mostly I remembered how much bigger he was than me; sitting next to him in front of the school, as we waited for our parents to pick us up, I would try to stretch myself over three steps just like him. I remembered asking him his shoe size as his feet seemed so much larger than mine. I remembered peeking at his math books, which were more complex than mine. André was older than most of the other children at our school but he sat in the same classes as we did. As I learnt in Boston, he didn't join an ordinary school until he was ten years old. Even then, his use of language was limited and sometimes he groaned very loudly when he could not express himself.

Fluency with language is a common problem for autistic children. The central objective of many of our lessons in Ms. Russell's class was developing our skills of conversation. There were always lots of toys at the school. But playing with those toys was not straightforward. We were regularly asked to talk about the game that we were playing or to try to describe the game that another child was playing. Games are very useful for developing language. Games rely on the making of categories, as does language. Games are based on the relationship of one thing to another, as is language.

For example, if you are faced with a square peg and a round hole, you will only try forcing the peg with your toy hammer for so long. Eventually, when you suffer this interruption, you have to explain, and in our case, it would be to a teacher, that the hole is 'not square', and that not only leads to a new word, 'circle', and an understanding for the first time of a firm difference between these two shapes, it provides an important realization: that the world may not fit into the categories that you already know about. In any case, negatives are an eloquent form of expression, providing opportunity for subtle distinctions. If you were walking through a deserted house after midnight, you wouldn't say to your friends, 'I'm fine'; you'd say, 'I'm not scared'.

Conversation is obviously essential to our lives, and to our minds. We form our views of ourselves, as well as our views about the world, in conversation with others. Yet the language that we use to conduct conversation is in itself a highly complex set of structures. We do not necessarily know this as children, but we know it as adults whenever we try to learn a new language. Autistic individuals, though, often know it even as children. They find the acquisition of language in any form very difficult. Conversation is harder still, for people say things in different ways, you need to comprehend tone and gestures as well as context and the words used in order to get to the meaning.

André had found an unusual way of overcoming his difficulties with conversation. For several years, he had been training as a puppeteer. He made his own puppets with wood and string. He put on shows in his neighborhood. And his use of the puppets was expanding. When he spoke on the telephone, one of the puppets was usually in his lap. He was a member of a chess club and he attended the meetings with Boo. He had been turned away from a speed-dating evening because he arrived with a new puppet he had just made called Sylvie.

The rule was that you couldn't interrupt one of his puppets. You could interrupt when André was talking – though there'd be a pause as he adjusted and you'd feel a little bit like you had stepped on his foot – but you certainly couldn't talk across one of his puppets. I had done it for the sixth time in the airport just as I was about to say goodbye to him and his sister. He had snatched my boarding card and disappeared.

'How long do you have?' asked Amanda.

'I'd like to be at the gate already,' I replied. She smiled and shrugged her shoulders.

★

I was introduced to Boo the first night that I arrived.

'This is Boo,' said André, as I peered into a glass of water that I had just poured from the tap.

'Don't drink that,' added Boo. I looked up. The voice was different. It wasn't an impersonation, he wasn't speaking with an added accent, or in a falsetto, but Boo's voice sounded different. André's voice was flatter in tone or it seemed to come from deeper down his throat. Amanda described it later as sounding like the inside of a bucket. André laughed at that. Boo's voice was no deeper or higher in its pitch, but it rose more often, especially at the beginning of words. André had told me about the puppets on the phone, before I arrived in Boston, but I hadn't guessed that he would introduce me so swiftly or that the voice would be different. 'Do you know the results of a chemical analysis that was conducted on a similar glass of water?' continued Boo. I shook my head.

'We won't start that,' smiled André, opening the fridge door with his other hand and indicating a filter jug.

'André?'

'Yes?'

'No, wait, Boo?' I was testing.

'Make up your mind, buddy,' exclaimed Boo. André grinned. It was hard to believe that he wasn't deliberately trying to make me feel uncomfortable for the sake of his own enjoyment.

'Give me one good reason why I shouldn't drink this glass of water,' I asked. 'Or one very much like it.'

'Arsenic,' replied Boo. 'Buddy, that's reason enough.'

'Really?'

'The arsenic content of tap water in American cities has been growing steadily. It's a scandal. There's more arsenic in that glass of water than in sixty per cent of light industrial waste.'

'Now that's not actually true, is it?' I countered.

Boo shook his head, conceding the point.

'You shouldn't have gotten him started,' remarked André with a smile. He shook the strings off his fingers and put the puppet down on the counter. Boo was well-made. Probably of birch. Quite small, no more than six inches tall. The strings were thin and colorless. He wore a hat and looked vaguely Amish. André poured me a glass of water from the jug in the fridge.

'You really don't drink tap water?' I asked. I wondered whether filtering the water was part of a routine. Autistic people often developed complex routines for straightforward tasks. Every time I showered, for example, I rubbed the different parts of my body in exactly the same order.

'I don't like the taste,' he replied, heading into the living-room. I followed.

*

I hadn't seen André in around twenty years. His father had been a banker for a long time, same as my dad, and they met up from time to time, whenever they happened to be in the same city, exchanged theories on oil prices and stories about corporate debt. But André and I hadn't met since I left the school in New York in 1984, at the age of seven, when my family moved away.

André stayed in the school for another six months, until

he turned ten, which was the point at which his parents decided that he couldn't be kept from the mainstream school system any longer. Even so, he had to join a private school and there was an extensive negotiation with the head teacher so that he started only a year behind where he would have been otherwise. He was good at math, reading, geography, fossils, the periodic table, the difference between Indian and African elephants, atomic weights, but he didn't speak very much. He was painfully shy, literally painfully shy, as he liked to play with paperclips and would drive an open paperclip under his nail for the duration of any sentence that he spoke. It helped him to focus, or it was an expressly mechanistic thing; as he described it, pushing the paperclip in, under his nail, forced out the words from his mouth.

During recess, he liked to walk around the school, running his finger along each of the window-sills that he could reach in the time before the bell rang for classes to resume. Sometimes his mother would come to visit him at lunch, and he'd sit in the car with her listening to the radio. Soon, he met Heloise, who didn't mind walking around the windows with him and didn't mind when she got teased alongside him. He still kept in contact with her. They agreed that they really didn't realize when they were at school that they were supposed to be miserable, that kids like them, with no friends, with odd habits, were supposed to have a horrid time, but they really didn't. They could tell a version in which they did – open pots of paint were placed in their schoolbags more than once; André frequently put his hand up, knowing the answer, but was then unable to say what it was, inviting the laughter of his classmates and the scorn of some of his teachers; Heloise once didn't make it to the toilets swiftly enough – but they didn't know that they were supposed to hate school and they didn't talk about it that way. They kept each other company and were good with books. They had supportive parents for when they came home.

André went on to study computer science. He excelled at it and was offered a research job straight out of college. I know computer scientists who do their programming from inside tubes made out of tin foil, who obliviously wear pants with embarrassing holes in them, who devote their living-rooms to experiments in super-cooling processor chips, or who can recite Ovid's *Metamorphoses* backwards, and none of them are autistic. Though I knew that André was autistic – seeing him sitting on a brown leather sofa with a wood frame that matched the finish of the coffee table, in a room with nice table lamps and a vase full of fresh flowers – he looked more normal than any of those computer scientists. Then I noticed that there were three more puppets on the coffee table and I noticed the content of the poster above his head. I recognized it immediately. It was a blown-up quotation from the *Diagnostic and Statistical Manual of the American Psychiatric Association*.

Before age three, the patient shows delayed or abnormal functioning in one or more of the following areas:

- Social interaction
- Language used in social communication
- Imaginative or symbolic play

I pointed to it. 'The poster?' I said.
'Oh, my sister put that up.'

'You don't mind it?'

'I don't mind it,' he replied. He picked up a puppet from the table.

'Why leave people to guess whether I am autistic or not? It's hardly a game,' pointed out the puppet, whose name, I later learned, was Ben-Gurion.

*

There were more posters. On the morning after I arrived, I woke late and didn't find André in the house. I was disappointed to get up late. I was anxious about staying in his house and had hoped to cook breakfast and complete other tasks. Now I had missed breakfast and André, my host, didn't seem to be around. I had worried about feeling like an intruder in the houses, workplaces and favourite cafés of my former classmates and it was happening already. It still surprised me that anyone agreed to let me visit them at all. André, though, was convinced really easily. I explained the concept of the book to him once and he said yes. I felt like I had tricked him, that I had put it in such a way as to obscure any of the difficulties that he may have wanted to raise. So I rang him again and explained it again and he said yes.

All that my parents had been able to tell me about André was that his parents had thought about putting him up for adoption after he was diagnosed with autism. Their marriage was fraying and they didn't think that they had the capacity to bring up an autistic child. It's possible that they never would have gone through with it anyway, it's possible that the adoption service would not have allowed it; however, on the night before their first appointment with a social worker, they both had epic nightmares. They woke with jittery limbs, gelled in sweat, and cancelled the appointment.

When I rang André a third time, I got his sister on the phone instead. Her name was Amanda. Amanda drove a cab and had moved in with her brother a couple of years ago, shortly after breaking off an engagement with a man who had been cheating on her for a year and a half. I asked her whether André had spoken to her about my visit. She told me that they'd heard about the book from their mother, who had heard about it from my mother, and this had happened even before I rang. She and André had talked about it and they were looking forward to meeting me. André's decisions were as good as anyone else's, I belatedly realized and booked a flight. But now neither André nor Amanda were anywhere to be found and my doubts were re-emerging. We hadn't said very much to each other the night before. Amanda wasn't around; I was tired; André was tired. We spoke a little about Boston. We went to bed early. I scanned my memory of our conversation for any bloopers but didn't find any.

After wandering around, from room to room, I pushed open a door in the kitchen. It led to the garage and, to my relief, I found André there. The walls were lined with framed posters. They had been created, André explained later, from course materials made available on the Internet by the Massachusetts Institute of Technology, a course on teaching computers how to talk. One of them read: 'We can think of grammars as a set of rules for rewriting strings of symbols: S > NP VP; NP > Name; NP > Art N.'

'I have moths,' remarked André as I walked into the garage. He had caught a couple and was looking at them on his desk. I peered over his shoulder. They were pretty big. 'There's a lot of them,' he added. He opened a clear plastic container that contained spools of wire and dumped its contents. He slid the moths into it gently with the palm of his hand. 'Will you help me catch some?' he asked. 'We need to work out where they live.'

I was still looking into the container. I had clenched my fists by my sides. One of the moths was much lighter in color than the other one and it was at least a centimeter longer. 'Those two are different,' I eventually said.

André brought them out again. 'You're right,' he admitted, returning one of the moths to the container. He emptied another container for storing the second one.

Though we took to the task energetically, we weren't especially successful at catching the moths. There weren't that many, or they had sensed that a cull had begun. We also had to stop each time one of us killed a moth and decide whether it was the same as one of those that we had already captured or whether it was a new type. Amanda returned from her taxi shift during this exercise and sat down at a computer to check her email. Within an hour, André had run out of plastic containers and his desk was littered with odd bits and nik-naks that had been removed to make room for new categories of moth. Boo hung off his left hand.

'We're doing fine,' commented Boo. 'We could do worse. If we tried, we could do worse. We haven't hit rock bottom just yet. We need to locate the origin of this blight. And . . .'

'I don't think moths live together,' I said, interrupting him. I was getting annoyed. I hadn't eaten anything. I was still wearing pyjamas. I had suggested three times that André was going to need to call an exterminator. As soon as I spoke, he barged past me, leaving the door into the kitchen open behind him. I looked around the garage, half-expecting to see a giant moth from whose vengeance André had fled so rapidly, but there was only Amanda, laughing in her chair.

'That's a prize expression on your face,' she remarked. 'So at least you didn't do that already last night. Well done.'

'Where did he go?' I asked.

'Don't interrupt the puppets,' she explained. 'It's not worth it. Don't do it if you're cross. Try not to do it accidentally. It makes him furious.'

'Why?'

'Oh, come on, you know why,' she replied, getting up from the desk.

'Because he's autistic? I don't think all autistic people have bad tempers.'

'Fuck it. Hey, do you want some breakfast?'

'I'm not challenging you. I'm just . . . maybe there's another reason.'

'Tell me when you know,' she shot back with a smile, over her shoulder.

I followed her into the kitchen. Amanda and her brother looked alike, except that if you were drawing a portrait of Amanda, you would use pastels. Her features were not as pointy as André's. Her complexion was milkier. The muscles in her neck didn't stand out so much. She talked to me about her fares from during the night. She and André had this discussion most days, I learnt. They crossed at breakfast, she coming in from work, he preparing to go out, and they'd talk about her fares. The night before, she'd had a man who had been in her taxi four times in the past month. She wondered if he was looking out for her and whether to drive past him the next time. She'd had two elderly men who played gin rummy across the backseat while she drove them across town. She'd had a woman who came in, cried for ten minutes, breaking off only to assure her to keep the meter running, that she'd certainly pay; when she was ready, she wiped her eyes, applied her make-up, handed over twenty dollars and left.

André didn't rejoin us until after we had finished breakfast. He came in and sat down without a word.

'I'm sorry,' I said.

André made no reply and looked away to his right. Just as I was about to repeat my apology, Amanda kicked me under the table. So I asked him about the posters instead.

André worked on a project developing artificial vision for computers and robots. The research had a huge number of possible applications, from bomb disposal through extraordinarily vigilant, networked surveillance systems that could follow a single figure across a town over the course of a day to monitoring apparatus for use in hospital wards. What André found most interesting about his research though was what he was learning about the difference between vision and language. This was why he had chosen the posters about artificial language. Language, he felt, needed to access, in his terms, a *dynamic* system whereas vision interfaced with a *static* system. You couldn't swap parts of a face around. And so a computer didn't need to spot radically different arrangements of the same face. A face was a complex object, sure, and while it may look different from different angles, that just meant ensuring that a computer picked up enough data to express the complexity, and model for different points of view. This was basically a technological challenge, of getting sufficiently high definition into the component that captured the image, and sufficiently high processor speed into the component that modelled it.

A face couldn't outright change. A spoken sentence though could change and still be the same sentence, that is, contain the same words, the same data, yet provide different emphases, connotations, and implications, or even a different overall meaning. It might not even have to change in its structure, it might just be said differently, by a different person, be accompanied by a raised eyebrow, or appear in a different place.

The problem is not that language is a complex system – which it certainly is. John McWhorter, author of *The Power of Babel: A Natural History of Language*, explains that languages have a tendency towards 'baroqueification' or generating more and more 'Dammit!' moments, as in, 'Dammit! How can anybody speak this every day?' He offers the example of Makah, a Native American language of the Pacific Northwest. In Makah, 'It's bad weather' translates as a single word, *wikicaxaw*. However, that word can then take a range of suffixes which allow the speaker to indicate where the information came from. Oh, and when a suffix is added, the final -w becomes a -k. Here are just three of the evidential endings:

wikicaxak-pid
'It's bad weather – from what it looks like' or 'Looks like bad weather'

wikicaxak-qad'i
'It's bad weather – from what I hear' or 'Sounds like bad weather'

wikicaxak-wad
'It's bad weather – from what they tell me' or 'They say it's bad out'

Obviously it isn't necessary for a language to develop these endings. English does fine without them, though it has other baroque and completely pointless features to compensate. However, it isn't the complexity of language, the array of suffixes, or the proliferation of rules for making plurals that causes difficulties for autistic individuals. In fact, the complexity probably helps. With complexity comes greater individuation. The more complexity, the less likely it is that the same word may mean two different things. The more rules and structures there are, the less an autistic individual has to rely on intuition and context to get the meaning of someone else's utterance. One meaning, one word would be the ideal. That's manageable.

As André confirmed, the problem wasn't complexity, it was the dynamism of language: that one word may have more than one meaning, or that you might convey a similar meaning in more than one way, each subtly different from the next.

Amanda interjected, chuckling, with the story of how André used to call women 'ladies' and how he would refer to girls as 'young ladies'. There was nothing inaccurate about his usage. But it also wasn't quite right. 'Ladies' just wasn't the term that you used, and referring to someone as a 'young lady' might get you laughed at or, worse, cause offense. Yet at other times, when speaking ironically, or as part of a joke, or accompanying a female friend to the theater, you might say 'lady'. But there were no rules for demarcating when it was OK and maybe even funny and when it was questionable or old-fashioned. You could try and write a set of rules but you'd find it pretty difficult and, anyway, you'd be missing the point.

This was why creating artificial language, getting computers to talk pretty, was so challenging. As one of André's posters put it, 'Natural Language Understanding (NLU) is about getting at the meaning of text and speech, not just pattern matching.' You can program a computer to match patterns, but it's a real struggle to produce code for intuition and sensitivity to context and so properly to create NLU, especially as we'd usually struggle to explain – in plain and comprehensive terms – even to ourselves how we arrive at the meaning of statements. For example, there can be nothing more excruciating than trying to explain the wherefore of a joke to someone who just didn't get it. Sometimes, after you've tried explaining it, you're no longer sure yourself that the joke was ever funny.

André too was good at pattern matching (S > NP VP; NP > Name; NP > Art N). He showed me tachometer readings at one point. Tachometers are sometimes placed in taxis or freight lorries and they record the movement of the vehicle: when it stopped, how long for, what speeds it travelled at, how fast it accelerated. Both he and his sister were really interested in tachometers, she because she drove a taxi, albeit one without such a device, and he because he was good at explaining them. He could pick out phases of high and low traffic, a series of traffic lights, where the driver had stopped for an amount of time that suggested he was picking up a fare. Getting at the meaning of text and speech was a more complex enterprise, however.

As André spoke about these differences between dynamic and static systems, I wondered about the role of the puppets. It seemed difficult for André, even still, to manage a dynamic system, that of language or conversation. And so, by using the puppets, it was possible that his aim was to multiply the number of roles he could adopt instead. Rather than moving around using the system, he had increased the number of places where he could stand. So when he didn't fully understand what someone else had said or when he couldn't properly express himself or when it was going to take too long to work out how to do so, he literally stopped being himself, shed the obligations of the role that he was already in and took a new one. Using the puppets he could also, for example, be ironic. When he wanted to say something ironic, he gave that line to one of the puppets. This way he wasn't saying something that wasn't literally true or contradicting something that he had said earlier; the puppet was doing it.

Amanda kicked me under the table for a second time. 'We should go out for a drink later,' she suggested.

André looked dubious, brushed something imaginary off his left shoulder quite firmly.

'Maybe somewhere quiet. I'll be a bit jet-lagged again tonight,' I replied, trying, as I saw it, to mediate between sister and brother.

Amanda nodded and smiled. She got up from the table. 'I'm going to sleep for a bit,' she explained, as she left the room.

André and I sat quietly for a couple of minutes, finishing our drinks. He put Boo back on his hand.

'Will you ring an exterminator?' Boo asked. I nodded.

*

I could hear Amanda calling my name from the other side of the house and so I knocked on the bathroom door again. Really, I should have banged my fist against it, kept banging, but my trepidation at being in another person's house was such that I could only knock, as if asking to be let in for an interview. I am a tall person but I don't behave like a tall person. For a long time, I slouched so deeply that I developed sciatic pains in my back and left leg. I frequently bump up against door frames and table edges as I underestimate the size of me. I am tall enough to interrupt conversations; when I sit up at the table, I should be able to draw attention. What constrains me – as well as good manners and modesty, which I hope not to lose – is what André may have been trying to overcome with his puppets. What if I draw someone's attention but then can't conceive of enough material to keep the conversation going? What if I get stuck? My confidence had improved sufficiently that I had come to André and Amanda's house but I did feel shy being there. I knocked at the bathroom door again, perhaps a little louder this time.

André had switched the light off from outside and about the only thing I could see was the flashing green LED on his electric toothbrush, indicating that it was now fully charged. Already, I felt spiteful and petty for not pulling out the plug and saving, for Amanda and him, the miniscule amount of electricity that the LED consumed. I knew that it was now past nine o'clock and this was why Amanda had come back into the house calling our names. We were supposed to have met her at the bar down at the end of the street at nine. This meant that I had been locked in the bathroom for about an hour. Perhaps André had left the house and gone somewhere else. Perhaps I had made him cross in a more serious way this time.

For the first fifteen minutes in the bathroom, I had stood against the radiator, warming my legs and then my back. I was sure that André would return and unlock the door and I was sure that I ought not to make a fuss about him locking me in. Amanda had warned me and I hadn't properly followed her instructions. Ben-Gurion had been explaining the scheme for the evening, setting out the options for where we might go; as he was talking, I had checked my watch and said: 'We'd better hurry.' That had been enough.

As the room began to feel stuffy, I started knocking on the door at brief intervals. I started calling out André's name. It was possible that Amanda would think we'd made other plans – we hadn't seen her since around 4 p.m. – and gone somewhere else. Sitting on the edge of the bathtub, I also realized that André must have pushed me. He didn't just pull the door shut, and put a chair against it, then turn off the light; he must have pushed me first, into the bathroom, as I had been standing on the threshold and not fully inside.

I stood up and, in the dark, tried to remove the door handle, but it was steadfast, screwed in tight. I scrabbled around in the cabinets for a screwdriver, for anything that, to my touch, might have the right sort of edge to substitute for one. Eventually, I gave up and laid out in the bath.

Despite being confined to a lavatory because of his temper over my interrupting one of his puppets, I couldn't help feeling that André's puppetry was perfectly reasonable. Conversation has the quality of performance and André, unable to engage fully in conversation in the ordinary course of events, made it into a more explicit sort of performance. Lying in the cold, plastic bathtub, locked in the dark, I remembered when I first realized that conversation was a form of performance.

I had been sitting with my college friends – this was in Glasgow – and I watched as they stopped being my friends. They changed the way they moved their hands. The manner in which they spoke changed. One of them started talking about some of the books that she had read as a child. I had spoken to her about some of these books before, but we had spoken about them book-by-book and what we remembered of them. But, this time, she said that there were three categories of books for young girls: books in which the heroine wore a pink dress, books in which she wore a blue dress, and books in which she wore dungarees. This wasn't what she had said before when we spoke about children's books. And it felt like she had invented these categories on the spot, but everyone then spoke as if these were the established categories and began to elaborate on some further features of each one.

As the conversation moved on, my friends suddenly revealed knowledge of fantastic and arcane domains and showed interest in things that I knew they weren't especially interested in, all for the sake of continuing the conversation. They managed ten minutes on bar mitzvahs though none of them were Jewish or had ever been to one. There was a further ten minutes on Inuit marriage rites which one of them had read an article on and these were compared to those of other traditions; the conversation moved on before any conclusions were offered.

As a child, I had regarded these exact traits as inauthentic – for example, the adult feigning interest in my comics – or damaging, because analysis should be thorough and it should be complete; they and the people possessing them were worthy of sulky contempt. But, after that afternoon watching my friends, I began to understand. A conversation is a performance. This is why it doesn't matter if we lose our unique tone of voice in conversation or appear different. Indeed, that's part of the point. Conversation requires insincerity. Or at least it is often indifferent as to whether a statement is sincere or insincere. What matters is whether it is funny, or disputatious, or revealing, or sad. It didn't matter that my friend didn't necessarily believe that all children's books for girls could be divided into three categories. It didn't matter if she made up that typology on the spot. It led to an entertaining discussion about children's books, it allowed people to remember other things about the books that they had read and, in a slightly more serious bent, even to criticize the books that are published for young girls: their limited range and the images of success that they peddle – be beautiful, charming and astute in a pretty pink dress or languish rugged and tomboy-ish in dungarees.

However, though conversation may well bring out matters of this sort, it shouldn't be directed at a conclusion and it shouldn't too firmly be about something. It should circle, it should break off, it should recommence at an entirely different point. If my friend had signalled that she wanted a conversation that sought specific recommendations on how to improve children's literature, I doubt that she'd have found any takers. Outside of formal settings such as meetings or conferences, a conversation is merely a series of juxtapositions. These juxtapositions musn't be aimed at establishing a particular collective point, they may do so, but that mustn't be the reason for them. I say something to you. A phrase in what I said, a topic, a point of view, or nothing at all connects with something that you contain. Then you say something. And like this, we proceed.

Most importantly perhaps, conversation is fun. And inauthenticity is fun. There is nothing wrong or immoral about trying to entertain people. In a conversation, it isn't necessary to connect absolutely or in depth with the feelings or views expressed by another. If the theme or subject matter of your story is close enough to the theme of the story told before, you are allowed to tell it. Put a series of these interventions together, come back to one theme, one phrase or one joke again and again; this is a conversation, it is enjoyable, and it can take up hours.

I didn't fully realize what I had learnt about conversation until I came to live and work in Cambridge. There were two dominant models of talking there, both different from that of conversation as performance. There was politeness: what do you study and what college do you study it at, how was your day, what did you read? And usually that was the prelude to the use of the second model, exchange of information: I'll tell you about peasant farming in Mongolia, if you tell me about the novel in nineteenth-century France. The art of conversation was not practised at all widely. At a dinner party, when the politeness ran out and if people felt that the occasion required them to refrain from exchanging information, that is, from talking about work, we played charades. We never played charades in Glasgow.

The problem with the academic intelligence that I was surrounded with in Cambridge was that it was too tidy. It reacted against insincerity, hyperbole, provocation and wordplay, which are all essential to the art of conversation. If the aim is to establish truth, then of course all of these elements must be disciplined. They threaten the project. But attaining truth is not the aim of most conversations.

Cambridge was also a highly competitive environment. It was hence always better to stay silent or speak reservedly, it was rarely advisable to begin talking about non-serious topics and it was never advisable to take the weaker position for the sake of doing something entertaining with it, or merely to keep the conversation going.

When younger, I used silently to condemn passengers who talked to strangers on buses or trains. Why can't they be alone with themselves? was my protest. Don't they have material enough in their heads to amuse themselves for this short trip? I understood their loquacity as a weakness. But since then I'd realized: they were the daring ones. They were constantly willing to perform. They wanted a new tightrope to walk across all the time.

A few weeks before coming to Boston to see André, I started a conversation with a stranger – in fact, two strangers. It's still rare for me. I feel confident and able, for the most part, to have conversations in formal settings – at work, when shopping in a store; there's an obvious point to most of those conversations and, say at work, I can employ my intelligence and my experience of tasks. I am also fine with friends and family, for I will see them again, and they know me already, so the consequences of failing in a particular conversation are slight. But talking to strangers is an undue risk. My first few lines will be the basis on which they decide whether to continue; they will evaluate me only on the basis of the conversation that we have; if I get stuck, it's too difficult to explain why. Striking up conversation with strangers is an autistic person's version of extreme sports.

Still, I do it from time to time. The two strangers I spoke to recently were seated next to me on a plane. They were an elderly Israeli couple. Fairly early on they explained, after having learnt that my parents were from Pakistan and that I had lived in the Middle East, that they were both anti-Zionists and they could never live in Israel again. I am roughly something like an anti-Zionist; I doubt that it's a good idea for a state to be formed entirely in accordance with the tenets of one religion. But, because I wasn't interested in having won the argument, because I was interested in having a conversation, I talked to them about the important elements of nationalism, of solidarity, and the notion of a homeland. I compared Israel to Pakistan. There are disanalogies between the two cases but this was a conversation, not an argument, so I didn't have to sort them out.

The couple resisted me for some time. But, gradually, they spoke about when they had originally moved to Israel, the relief it gave them. They spoke happily about living in a kibbutz. They spoke about their children's experiences of Israel, especially of military service. One had enjoyed it, one had not. They spoke about friends who still lived in Israel, their insecurities, their qualms. I had a lovely time on that flight. I also acquired many stories for use in other conversations. As George Meredith put it, 'Anecdotes are portable; they can be carried home, they are disbursable at other tables.' I also just plain learned a lot. My understanding of the issues became more sophisticated. And this happened exactly because I treated the situation as a conversation, and not as an argument. And we didn't hold forth like it was an exchange of information either; we made it into a performance, into an event in itself.

It is the sort of conversation that I had with the couple on the plane that typically gets political philosophers excited. There is a strand of thought which holds that a political system prospers from conversation. Jürgen Habermas wrote that if we were all inserted into an 'ideal speech situation' (the economy cabin of a 747?), we would ultimately come to a consensus on any issue. At the very least our disagreements would be clarified, misunderstandings would be removed. The promise of such rewards becomes the premise for proposals for institutionalized, democratic conversations in 'deliberative forums' or 'virtual town halls'.

It may be that such proposals are flawed because we actually wouldn't all end up agreeing or making progress with 'our issues'. Perhaps if the man and woman on the plane had been ardent Zionists, we would have retreated into the in-flight entertainment quite quickly, or we would have gotten into a quarrel and asked to be moved from our seats. One version of this thought is captured in Thomas Hardy's remark that 'argument is powerless against bias or prejudice.' A nobler version suggests that different traditions contain different conceptions of reason and substantiate different forms of experience and knowledge with the result that certain disagreements may well be intractable. Is there any-

32

thing that an agnostic who has been through the mill with a terminally ill parent can say to a committed Catholic on the subject of euthanasia?

A further problem with such models of democracy may be that they conceive of conversation not as a performance but as a process. The point of the conversation is stipulated – it is agreement. Would we want to take part in such a conversation? Would the fun still be there? I know a lot of people who would love to take part in these conversations, but only because they have such truth-directed conversations all the time and only because they know they are good at them – they are policy advisors or academics. Would the rest of us want to have a conversation with them? If we disagreed with them, would they open themselves up to being convinced by us? The thing about conversational democracy may be that the people who are good at the art of conversation might be rotten conversational democrats. The ones who would prosper would be those who are good at argument. And those who are good at argument, the logical, the single-minded, the dominating types, well, don't they often have terrible opinions?

That isn't to say that the art of conversation – the performative ideal that André, with his puppets, in some sense embodied – has no political implications. I can still get excited about the potential of the conversation on the plane, but for a different reason. What may be politically valuable about conversation is the insincerity it encourages. My parents' friends had no interest in what comics I read, but it was good that they asked me. Their effort was important. My effort, in trying to convince the Israeli couple to be Zionists again, was important. Conversation flourishes when we entertain each other. Conversation flows when we, each of us, flit between different points of view. Conversation sometimes requires us to ask questions, the answer to which we are not interested in ourselves, but which we feel the other person might enjoy or appreciate the opportunity to provide. Conversation, in short, promotes civility. And a society that is marked by deep disagreement and characterized by a high level of heterogeneity should certainly place a high value on civility. It may not be possible for us to agree. But it may be possible for us to disagree entertainingly and be able to disagree in ways such that we can see and even expound each other's point of view.

André's different puppets didn't quite instantiate different points of view, or, so far as I could tell, entirely different aspects of his personality (i.e. Boo wasn't the sum of all his mischievousness and he could be sociable without Sylvie), but I expected there was probably some pattern as to why he used one puppet at certain times and a different one at other times. I had hoped that going out with him, seeing which puppet, or puppets, he took with him, and how he used them when out, would help me to work out the correlations; but, still trapped in the bathroom, I was beginning to think that Amanda had despaired of us and gone on somewhere else, and that André might not relent until the morning. I had just introduced this unappealing thought to myself when I heard the front door slam and Amanda's voice call first for her brother and then for me.

Gradually, her voice came closer and nearer, and my knocking grew bolder. She reached the bathroom and knocked from the outside. I knocked back. I heard her begin to laugh, an ascending laugh, a laugh of proper delight.

I sat down cross-legged on the floor just behind the door and joined in while she withdrew the chair and opened the door.

'Come on,' she beckoned, and we began to look for André.

We found him in the living-room. He was sitting behind one of the sofas, his back against its side, Ben-Gurion in his lap. 'I need to stop doing that,' I said. I meant it. Sustaining the performance was a difficult thing for André to do. He couldn't do it alone, he needed to use the puppets, and he needed the help of those he spoke with. Maybe the extent of his anger was excessive, certainly sitting in a clammy bathtub I had felt it was disproportionate, but I could grasp the root of it. I remember sitting in a public lecture, a couple of months before I had gone to Boston, and that I had to leave after fifteen minutes. I disagreed with too much of what the speaker was saying, I was finding it hard to store all the disagreements, and I knew that I wouldn't be able to stand up at the end and make all the points I'd like to make; even if I was selected to ask a question, I'd start talking, realize that I was doing so in front of an audience, some of whom may disagree with me, or think me annoying, and I would curtail my comments immediately. I am a mild person but I could identify no option bar leaving the room. Often, at work, when I have a run of meetings, I need to leave one early so that I can go and sit in a lavatory cubicle for a couple of minutes, or dash outside. Perhaps everyone feels like doing that sometimes. For me, it's not because I'm frustrated or tired, I do it because I feel that I am performing; I have to consider how I'm going to act in the next meeting, what my objectives are, because otherwise I may not be able to do it.

Amanda and I stood silent for three beats. Then André

got up and gave me a brief hug. Thus reconciled, we went out.

'Look, I hear what you're saying about the importance of Hector,' conceded Ben-Gurion, 'but you can't seriously defend a film with a soundtrack so bad.'

People exhibited a range of different expressions when André produced his puppet – in this case, to try to win an argument about the film *Troy*. I kept looking over at Amanda whenever Ben-Gurion emerged from André's coat, expecting her to look embarrassed, or poised to intervene, but she just seemed interested. Interested in other people's reactions. Interested in what her brother, via the puppet, was saying. Interested in what I might be thinking. Just interested. And, watching her interest, I began to relax too. Initially, I had expected hostility. I had expected people to yell 'weirdo'. Even that some places might throw us out.

'Did you make that yourself?' asked a woman standing close by. André nodded.

'Wow. That's amazing. It's so detailed.'

'His name is Ben-Gurion,' added André.

'What sort of wood is it?' It turned out that the girl's grandfather had been a carpenter. She began telling André about her memories of him and his work. André told her about making the puppets. Amanda and I talked among ourselves.

'Has anyone ever made trouble about it?' I asked her, once André had gone to the bathroom. 'Has anyone ever snatched a puppet from him when you're out like this, for instance?'

Amanda nodded. 'It's happened a couple of times.'

'Does he get angry?'

'He's timid when he's outside. Only a lion when he's at home. That's a saying, isn't it?'

'What happened those times?'

'I was surprised,' she admitted.

'Why?'

'Both times, other people — strangers, this is — got the puppet back.'

'They did?'

'Of their own accord. We didn't have to make any fuss. I'm not sure we would have. Now, I would. Because I feel that people will help. When it happened the first time, I was probably going to stay quiet and leave without making a scene. But it didn't happen like that. Two guys, who saw it happen, confronted the other guy — they didn't know him, he was being a prick — and got the puppet back.'

'Did you talk to them afterwards?'

'Sure. We said thank you and that sort of thing.'

'What did they say?'

'One of them asked André if he was autistic. André said "yes". They talked about that for a bit.'

I was about to keep going when André returned. He sat down and brushed something off his sister's shoulder. 'I was telling him about the first time someone grabbed Boo from you. I was telling him you fought off four guys, six foot each, to get him back.'

André paused. I felt that Amanda had made a misjudgment. I wondered if she was tipsy. I felt sure that it was a bad idea to remind André of the incident. 'There was five of them, wasn't there?' replied Ben-Gurion. Then André began laughing.

Over the course of the evening, we developed a rule that whenever someone started a compulsive activity, someone else slapped his or her hand. Amanda was less prone to it than André or I. For example, I began introducing extra bends into a straw at one point, really focussing on this quite hard, and Amanda slapped my hand just before André could. We kept score. André led throughout though I wasn't far behind. It was 15–10–4 by the end. I got Amanda once as she tugged on her right sleeve. She complained that this wasn't compulsive. I pointed out that she did it roughly every five minutes. André got hit by both of us each time he brushed something off one of his shoulders and Ben-Gurion adjudicated as to who got in first.

Earlier, I mentioned the way that autistic people regularly seek local coherence. Craig's refrain of 'Send in the Idiots' was an example of it. I rarely go out without a crocodile clip in my pocket though recently my cell phone has begun to substitute for it. I play with it for something to focus on while I try to do something harder, like explain to a friend why I didn't return her call. I noticed, as the night progressed, that André looked for local coherence only when Ben-Gurion was not part of the conversation. He ran his finger repeatedly along the edge of the bar. He spun the ice in his glass. He brushed imaginary things off his shoulders.

One of the bars we went to had a sign that read: 'No Dogs Allowed'. This was a statement of a rule. The strategies that autistic individuals use to negotiate the world of others – for example, when making trips to bars – are also like rules. Like all rules, the barkeeper's rule had some problems. For instance, it was over-inclusive. The purpose of the rule was to prohibit the entry of animals that might be a nuisance.

Not all dogs are a nuisance though and so the rule covered animals that it didn't need to cover in order to achieve its purpose. The rule was also under-inclusive. Though its purpose was to prohibit the entry of animals that might be a nuisance, clearly there were animals other than dogs that might be a nuisance. Despite these problems of form though, the rule probably tended to work. It achieved local coherence. We could make sense of it. There may have been a confrontation if someone turned up with their pet bear but, on the whole, the rule did what it was supposed to do.

The strategies that autistic individuals adopt can be similarly successful. After my family moved from New York, I attended an ordinary school. There was one other autistic child, a girl a year older than me. A teacher told me about her – a teacher, I remember, who had been informed that I was autistic and kept expecting me to do something extraordinary in class, like finding a new sub-atomic particle while we made macaroni pictures, or reciting entire chapters of books from memory when we studied English, and was disappointed when I didn't.

I began to spot the girl at lunchtimes. I think she had been told the same thing about me – 'He's just like you'. We were shy of each other. We never became friends. However, I remember that when many of the kids in the school went through a spate of swapping items from their packed lunches – a perplexing time for me, during which I often ended up with pumpkin seed bread and flapjacks – she sought to fill her lunchbox with foods beginning with the same letter of the alphabet. If she chose 'B', for example, she'd give away her apple for a banana. She'd tell people what her letter was for the day and then there would be a basis for swapping. Of course, her rule was over-inclusive, because there might be foods beginning with the letter she had chosen that she didn't like, and it was under-inclusive because she might really want a cheese sandwich above all else but her letter for the day was 'B'. Nevertheless, while I would get flustered amid the swapping, soliciting and deal-making, she was fine because she had a rule.

In a bar, though, local coherence might be quite difficult to attain. What is the purpose of going to a bar? The barkeeper who wants to keep dogs out has a single purpose and can use a rule to achieve it. The girl with the alphabetized lunchbox wanted some items that she didn't mind eating and could choose a letter of the alphabet that made that possible. Going to a bar, however, probably bears several purposes. The purpose is to have a good time. The purpose is to meet friends. Or to make friends. It's easy enough to say what the rule about keeping dogs out of bars is supposed to do, but what are you supposed to do in a bar?

It's also that any one answer may conflict with the other possibilities. Part of the purpose may be to have a good time, but does this mean that if you are not enjoying the company of your friends you don't need to talk to them? Probably not. Or probably you don't need to talk to them for the entire time, but you do need to talk to them a bit. Hence the purposes get mixed up. And local coherence becomes already a bit harder to achieve.

The other problem with something like going to a bar is that you're not in control. The barkeeper can keep dogs out of his establishment. The girl who was 'just like me' could shut her lunchbox if she wasn't getting her way. But, if you adopt a rule like 'only talk to people wearing green', you can't compel green-wearers to talk to you. In fact, the outing might go especially badly if you explain to people that the reason why you sidled over is that they are wearing green and you're only talking to people in green outfits. And what might you do if someone other than a greenie tries to talk to you?

So the problem of local coherence is left outstanding. André's solutions – playing with the ice in his glass, making a pattern on the bar with his fingertips – were not high-tech, but they effected a narrow, uncomplicated purpose, and he was in control. He couldn't pull the entire bar-going experience into a coherent ball of dough, but he could do these other, much less ambitious things, and when he did them everything else became background. He could talk to people who were wearing red.

This is called local coherence. And gaining local coherence can be relatively easy. Certainly André made it look like it was.

And yet, Ben-Gurion had to come out from time to time. The best opportunities to observe André and his use of the puppet came when Amanda was talking. At one point she was describing how, after breaking up with her fiancé, she entered a brief obsessive phase during which she bought digests about guns and lengths of rope and she frequently sat at home flicking through the pages, comparing different guns, or making nooses out of the rope. It was a discomfiting account to listen to, especially for a brother. And I watched as André began trying out micro-behaviours, simple attempts to coherentize, like playing with the zip on his coat pocket, or wiping the outside of his glass in circular motions with his thumb and pinkie. But then Ben-Gurion came out, and not only did André begin to look more at ease but also he began to ask his sister questions by using the puppet. These were questions that sought to make the situation lighter. Ben-Gurion asked what types of rope she had bought and how he had often flirted with the notion of joining the National Rifle Association himself. Amanda ignored some of this but, quite deliberately, it seemed to me, helped out her brother by responding to some of the questions.

Later on, she also spoke about their father. They never saw much of him. He wanted to work as a missionary, perhaps especially so after having spent much of his life as an investment banker. He learnt Spanish and went to Brazil. Realized his mistake and moved to Argentina. He got cancer eventually and returned to the US before he was unable to. They got to know him a little, in hospital rooms, over the last month of his life. Though André certainly had a part in this story, he didn't join her in telling it. He became agitated instead and began to stroke his stomach. Ben-Gurion then started interrupting again.

It seemed that the puppets came out when André couldn't find local coherence. He tried for that first. But when he couldn't get it, he substituted one of the puppets for his own self. He escaped instead of standing there without local coherence. This was what the puppets gave him, a powerful back-up to the more conventional resources of the autistic individual.

I wondered if it was still hurtful for Amanda, being unable to share such an account with her brother, or whether she had educated herself not to feel that way any more. She lived with him but there were sharp limits to their intimacy. The puppets kept intervening, especially when she raised something difficult, precisely something on which she might need his help, when it might be useful to hear his version of it. And, once the puppets intervened, she wasn't allowed to speak across them. She wasn't allowed to be spontaneous, cross, or frustrated. Or she could be. But he would fly out of the room. Between André and anyone else, including Amanda, there was this barrier to intimacy – all conversation had to retain this element of method at all times.

The evening ended in André and Amanda's back garden. We found two of her colleagues, quite by chance, and they came back with us to the house. Amanda melted cheese slices on toast and we sat outside eating and chatting. André put on a brief puppet show. He prefaced it with lots of announcements about it being provisional and that he was still writing it and that he may never perform it properly; but then he gave us snippets of it. It featured Boo and Sylvie. So far as I could tell, it was something he had written himself.

In the play, Sylvie was Boo's daughter. Boo bought her some building blocks but, by the time he got home, she was asleep. He was disappointed that she was asleep and he tried to wake her up gently – standing beside her, yawning loudly – but she was in a deep sleep and snoring. He left her side and became interested in the building blocks. He started making something out of the blocks. It was hard to tell what it was but it was tall rather than round. Also, once the fact that Sylvie was snoring had been introduced, there was a break in the action every ten seconds or so and André made a snoring sound. This act of the play ended when Boo's construction came to life and slipped away. Boo became very worried that he had spoiled the special present he had bought and set off in pursuit.

Everyone applauded and André looked very pleased. For the first time during the evening, he shook himself free of any puppets and sat down on the grass. I went into the kitchen with Amanda to get the last of the melted cheese toasts and she warned me not to ask him anything else about the play. I had planned to. I was surprised by the play. The puppets, I had thought, were a coping mechanism. And yet here these same puppets were being used as a mode of expression. Something creative was being done with them, not just something therapeutic. But she asked me not to ask him anymore and I agreed. Anyway, it was very late and André looked calm, almost like he was sitting at the bottom of a swimming pool, momentarily enjoying the feeling of being immersed in cool water and the silence there in the depths.

After we'd finished eating, we all decided to sleep outside. Amanda brought out an electric heater and André and I helped her carry out sleeping bags and a couple of old duvets that he had once bought in a yard sale. André and I settled down side by side. He began talking about his work again. He explained that the research that was being done on getting computers to understand sign language was one step in developing artificial vision. Researchers foresaw that there were variances between how different people signed the same letters or words and so, rather than programming computers to recognize closely-defined patterns, they sought to develop understanding of sign language through programming them to pick out particular reference points. Different people may sign the same word in slightly different ways but there must be enough similarity between the different methods for other people to know that the same word is being signed. Unfortunately, for developers of artificial vision, these similarities were very difficult to identify. Even in understanding signed speech, people rely on context and intuition much more than the researchers had hoped. Finding applications for artificial vision was going to be hard work as whenever we apply our vision, we complement it with other sense data that are much tougher for a computer to decipher.

As André spoke, I tried to work out whether he was telling me this as a way of explaining his own difficulties with language or whether he was telling me this because it was an interesting and central problem in his research. I tried to think of him at work. I wondered whether in a laboratory of computer scientists his autism and use of puppets was understood as an eccentricity, of the same genre as working inside a cone made of tin foil, like another friend of mine who was a computer scientist. Or whether other people in his lab thought about the puppets and his use of them in conversation, much as I was trying to, and wondered what it told them about the challenges in their work.

I wasn't allowed to go to the lab with him. Amanda had been very strict about that in an email she sent before I arrived in Boston. I had worried in advance that, if everyone shut me out of parts of their lives like this, I wouldn't be able to complete this book. In fact, I told Amanda that in my reply. Having already spent a night in their house and after the evening we had just spent together, however, that seemed like a misplaced concern. After breakfast the next morning, it was going to seem ridiculous – there was no hiding going on. Anyway, Amanda had explained that she didn't go to André's lab either. She felt that he needed a space that was his own, where he didn't have to contend with her help or my analysis.

So I let him finish talking about his work and then we gradually wound down, looking up at the sky, its seams just beginning to crack to reveal the morning light, quick-quizzing one another about recent missions to space. I don't remember which one of us fell asleep first.

*

We reassembled the next morning over breakfast, murmuring about our hangovers. We rubbed our heads a lot and drank a lot of water. While André made pancakes in the microwave, I checked whether Amanda's interdiction from the night before about the puppets had run its course. She nodded and so, as I made eggs and Amanda mixed juices, I asked André about when he had started to learn about puppets. Was there a book that he read? Did he see a course advertised?

He didn't reply immediately. After a moment of familiar silence, he tried to change the subject, started telling me about a job interview he attended with Boo: the receptionist who tried to send him away; the professor who saw him anyway then declared at the end that he'd come across people who lied about their grades, described unwritten articles as 'forthcoming', and that – since there was really no way of ascertaining, after a brief interview, who the best or most able candidate was, who would be reasonable to work with – he'd give the job to André because he had used a new trick – a puppet – to make his impression. André left that job after six months, when the professor married a past graduate student and left on a year-long honeymoon with the result that the sponsors of the project pulled out.

Amanda waited until André got to the end of his story. 'He met someone who was into puppets,' she said in his stead. André cleared his throat and concentrated on eating again. 'They got to be quite close friends.'

'This was someone from work?' I asked André. He shook his head.

'He met this guy in a place for juvenile offenders,' continued Amanda. I stopped eating and looked up at her. 'André was there for a year.' I glanced over at André. He had pushed his plate away and was holding on to the edge of the table with both hands as if trying to prevent it from sliding into his stomach. 'André had a milkshake in his hands and this guy bumped into him,' Amanda began to explain, 'and it might not have been by accident, it might have been done out of meanness. Anyway, André started hitting him. The milkshake went over his front and he lost his temper. He started hitting this guy. Put him to the floor. And really kept going. Some neighbors had to drag him off.' She paused for a moment and took a sip from her glass. 'It took a long time to sort out, but we were very lucky that the DA didn't press for attempted murder. André destroyed this boy. He beat his head against the pavement. There was internal bleeding. Hemorrhage. A lot of it came down to André's medical reports.'

Amanda sighed, lifted up her plate and put it on the counter behind her. She gazed out of the kitchen window at the garden we had spent the night in. The sleeping bags were out on the line to dry out from the dew. I felt dizzy. I hadn't known anything like this had taken place. André was crying.

I tried to reach out and put a hand on his shoulder but he shirked from me. He got up and left the room.

'Why did you do that?' I demanded. Amanda kept silent. 'I didn't need to know that. You could have told me when he wasn't here.'

'He should be reminded,' she replied. 'Kamran, he needs to know. He almost killed someone. He can't be allowed to forget that. It's too serious.' She spoke urgently and fixed her stare on me as soon as she finished, holding me until I offered some reaction. It took me almost a minute.

'You're the only one who can do that,' I realized. She turned and looked back out of the window. We sat in silence for a while and then got up and cleared the dishes. I washed them as Amanda went to look for her brother.

*

Amanda and I stood by the balustrades, watching people walk up and down the airport concourse, searching for one another, checking the departure boards. André still hadn't returned and my flight had started boarding. Neither Amanda nor I wanted to go to the flight desk and explain what had happened so I decided that I would forfeit the cost of the flight and book another one for later in the day. Amanda insisted that André earned really good money now and that I should make him pay for it. But I doubted that I would. I wanted to feel furious. But I couldn't. I wanted to believe, as Amanda had suggested, that perhaps he wanted me to stay a bit longer and this, though it had begun in anger, had become friendlier, a bit of a joke. But I couldn't. So I was left standing there, watching the fluid movement of traffic through the airport, shaking my head from time to time, chatting to Amanda.

When I had first arrived, I had expected that the puppets were something like media for André's sense of fun, that he struggled with conversation on his own, but that, through the puppets, he had found access to the notion of conversation as performance. I wished that was so. Watching his show in the garden, late at night, it had still seemed that it might be.

We do so much through conversation. We try to make each other laugh. We build plotlines. We share ideas. And, perhaps equally importantly, we criticize and analyze, even effect small meannesses. The other thing about conversation – what André, I felt, ought to have access to, probably more than anything else – is its spontaneity. Through conversation, we find ourselves reaching views and trying out ideas that we wouldn't otherwise get to. Very few people write, which can be equally useful in this regard. André didn't write. And so, for André, as for most people, conversation offered the only proper escape from himself.

We recognize that this is what conversation achieves. You've said something during an argument, perhaps even vehemently, that you didn't hitherto know you had in you. You've told a story that you had forgotten. This isn't always a good thing. And I'm reluctant to say that the power of conversation is in reaching authenticity. After all, you've also regretted what you said during an argument. And revised it. Gone back to it, apologized for it, wondered where it came from.

Still, there is something powerful here and I had hoped that André would know about it, if only through the puppets. It's because of the spontaneous nature of conversation, for example, that debates are more interesting than speeches. The US presidential elections provide perhaps the best illustration of this. Stump speeches are important, and when they're done well they do tell you something about the character of the candidate. But debates are better. As so often with US politics, it's the drama series, *The West Wing*, that provides the best illustration of this.

President Bartlett is running for re-election against Governor Ritchie. The parallels to Gore vs. Bush in 2000 are entirely non-accidental. Ritchie is a charismatic conservative, running a good campaign, slick, shoring in his base, tempting voters in the moderate heartland. Bartlett, on the other hand, though he is the incumbent, is perceived as professorial, proud, clever, liberal, out of touch with traditional values. On the eve of the only debate of the campaign, polls show the two candidates virtually neck and neck. Prior to the debate, Bartlett has spent forty-eight hours at 'Debate Camp', hunkering down with his advisors, honing his lines. He gives a good performance but Ritchie does too. Then, towards the close of the debate, a question is asked about crime, perhaps the most touchstone of touchstone issues, and Ritchie delivers a fantastic answer – short, precise, quotable. It's now Bartlett's turn. He pauses. The camera roves in. And Bartlett says:

> There it is. The ten-word answer. My advisors have been looking for the ten-word answer all week. It's supposed to be the key to an election. But I have a question for Governor Ritchie. What are the next ten words?

It's a gloriously arrogant response. What makes it better is that, earlier in the episode, we have watched Bartlett's advisors try to come up with their own version of the ten-word answer. They've been striving for it, and failing. So it's not that Bartlett is dismissing the stratagem itself. Instead he's saying, 'Can you manage conversation?'

Put yourself on the spot. Trust yourself. Say the next thing in your head. Tell me, what are the next ten words? That's the challenge of conversation. You need the next ten words. And you have no time to prepare them. Bartlett is telling Ritchie, and the American electorate, that he knows that Ritchie's advisors came up with the ten-word answer. Bartlett's own advisors were trying to do it for him. Does Ritchie have his own answer though? This is partly, 'Are you smart enough?' but, more importantly, it's, 'Are you any good at talking?' Bartlett has just done it, he's just spoken, unscripted, untrammelled, and suddenly it's Ritchie who looks out of touch, not only because he doesn't have more than the ten words written by his advisors with which to connect to the concerns of voters, but because he doesn't trust his instincts. He's the phoney now, not Bartlett.

As Ritchie admits to Bartlett at the end of the debate, whispering it to him as they shake hands, 'You killed me tonight.' Bartlett shed the carapaces added by his advisors and the commentariat and just made conversation. And Ritchie couldn't do the same.

André can't do the same either. He can't escape. He can't soar. Not even with the puppets. Instead the puppets, rather than a means of emancipation, are a further defense against the breach of his local coherence. So he tries, as I saw him do when we were out, first of all, to reach local coherence, to protect himself by putting the more complex things into the background and focussing instead on tapping a pen against the surface of a table or lining up empty glasses. When that fails, the puppets are the next aspect of his strategy. And when the puppets fail, when someone talks over one of his puppets, when the local coherence that he has already tried so hard to attain seeps away, he loses his temper, suddenly, straightaway, with no pause for reflection.

There would be another way to deal with the first breach of local coherence. He could bring the things that he tried to cast into the background back to the fore. He could properly admit defeat, struggle with the gunk of life just like the rest of us. But he doesn't do that. Instead, when confronted by strong emotion or discomfiting experience, he brings out a puppet. He goes to the backup technique. And he first developed this technique when he was put in an institution for beating someone's skull repeatedly against stone.

But Amanda didn't want to talk to me about this as we waited for her brother in the airport. I wasn't going to learn anything more about his time in prison. And I didn't want to fixate on it either. So we stood there, peering through the concourse, watching the light shift as the sun set, spotting changes of staff in the shops and kiosks, hellos and goodbyes, how long people waited after dropping someone off, did they cross their arms and sigh, did they stand and watch other people for a little while or did they breathe in hard and walk off towards the rest of their lives?

2

'SPECIAL DELIVERY,' CHIRPED RANDALL'S alarm clock every morning as he woke at 4.30 a.m. to get set for work. He tried to switch it off before it spoke again. He kept his work clothes in a room down the hall, showered in that en-suite, all to avoid waking his partner, Mike. Mike kept to a very different regimen. He usually worked best late at night, after Randall had gone to bed. He was writing his first novel and sometimes didn't get to sleep until an hour before Randall was due to get up. They had decided that it was important to share a bed though, and so both had learnt how to move carefully in the dark and to give the other person a gentle hug on leaving or entering the bed, enough to promote a feeling of closeness but not to wake him.

After getting ready, Randall ate two pieces of fruit, wearing his bag, standing by the kitchen window looking at the rear garden. He strapped on his cycle helmet and then got into the starting position of a sprinter. He checked his watch, waited until the second hand was on the 3, 6, 9 or 12, and then bolted. He took his bike from its stand by the garage, ran alongside it for three or four strides, leapt on and started pedaling. He rode down the middle of each street, his eyes closed, counting until he knew it was time to make a turn. He and Mike lived in a suburb of Chicago and the commuters weren't active until much later in the morning. When there was the occasional aberrant vehicle, Randall heard it, a distinct noise amid the steady hum of the streetlights, and heard it well enough to discern where it was and what direction it was taking.

He opened his eyes reluctantly as he glided out of the residential streets but, despite Mike's suspicions, insisted that he wasn't waiting until later and later each morning before doing so. As he got closer to the city, the sunrise got closer too, and the sounds became more variegated. From the soprano of the streetlights, and the percussion of the occasional sprinkler system left out during the summer, the sky filled with the howls of trucks and the harrumphs of cars. Randall liked the sounds of the city though. They made him feel calm, because other things, outside of him, were always happening. The sounds felt like they formed a net and that, even if he did close his eyes again, he would land safely.

It took him around an hour to get into work. He was usually the first rider to arrive. He worked as a courier. His routine was to park his bike, eat a doughnut from the pack that the supervisor bought each morning, rub the balm that Mike's mum mixed for him into his legs and then help the supervisor organize the packages for the day. The company he worked for held a number of contracts with interstate and international couriers for the business districts of Chicago. They also took their own calls for work within the city. And, as a consequence, because the different companies had different service standards and different delivery times, sorting out the packages and itineraries for the riders was a tricky task. The supervisor was a much older man and he appreciated Randall's help. They worked together in silence until they were done and then shared a pot of coffee and more doughnuts before the riders started arriving and they, together with Randall, set out for the morning.

Randall did his job well, though, from time to time, he made mistakes. He didn't feel able to stride up to a reception desk when it was busy and remained standing to one side until the crowd at the desk thinned out. Sometimes this took five or ten or twenty minutes; if this happened a couple of times during a morning, he started missing delivery deadlines. He also didn't like to ride his bike unless all the sounds and textures were right. If the brakes were a little off, or the chain wasn't spinning as easily as it might, he got off the bike, took out his tools and meddled with the parts. In this way too, he sometimes began missing deadlines. He knew that it was important to meet deadlines – it made him anxious to even come close to missing them – but he became edgier still if his bike wasn't right. He would lose his ability to maneuver through traffic, forget short cuts, become unable to fit new packages that customers handed him into his day's schedule. Whenever he had a bad day though, the supervisor spoke up for him. That wasn't why Randall arrived before the other riders in the morning, but it was why the supervisor didn't stop him from doing so.

Usually, the couriers never found out what was in the packages. Sometimes a person would be so eager to receive the delivery that he would open it straightaway and the rider would see the contents, or a package set for pick-up wouldn't quite be ready; but usually the packages were just packages, with anonymous contents, distinguished from one another only by shape or size or the handwriting or typescript used on the label. On the day that I arrived in Chicago, however, Randall got to see the insides of two of his packages.

The first one was his very first delivery of the day. It was often his first delivery of the day, to a law firm close to the Sears Tower. Randall knew the building well; he knew which receptionists worked on which days and when the partner, who sometimes asked to receive the package personally, took his annual holiday in Alaska. That morning, Randall was motioned through to the partner's office. The partner stayed behind his desk, maintaining that he just needed to send this email and would Randall open the package while he waited for the signature, just so that he could be sure that it was what he was waiting for. Randall hesitated – he'd never been asked to do this before – and then opened the package very carefully. Inside it was a green wool sweater. He pulled it out and put it down on the table. When he looked up, the partner was grinning. 'I hope it's the right size,' he said. 'The girls out front thought it would be.'

The second set of contents that he saw, he saw before they were put into a package. Often he picked up packages at the same time as he dropped others off. Later that morning, he made a delivery to another regular client, the owner of a pornography store, who thanked him and then put a gun down on the table. 'Can you deliver this for me? Across town?' he asked.

Randall explained that all pick-ups had to be phoned into the office. His client said fine and made the call, breaking off to test the weight of the gun in his hand and provide his estimate to Randall's supervisor on the other end. He then slipped the gun into one of the packages that Randall's firm supplied to regular customers and handed it to him.

'Did he tell your guy it was a gun?' I asked, as we sat waiting for the film to begin in Mike and Randall's local cinema. They always went to the cinema on a Wednesday night and I was happy to be invited to join them.

Randall shook his head. 'I think that we don't usually ask when it's a regular customer. We know what their packages are.'

This reply manifested the same literalness that I knew André evinced. André spoke, for example, about a neighbor who, soon after he first moved into his house, challenged him one evening as he was walking up to his own front door. André showed him his key and the incident didn't escalate. The man walked off, remarking, 'It's just that there's not many ethnics living around here.' Amanda and I were outraged when he told us this story, wanted to know who the man was, which house he lived in. But André didn't get it. The man hadn't been rude to him. He was glad that people were vigilant about protecting the neighborhood. And, it was true: he and Amanda were the only 'ethnics' on that street.

It couldn't be described as innocence. André had come across racist attitudes before. He had been abused more openly before. It wasn't that he carried around a happy, smiley conception of the world. Randall, similarly, knew to ask whether the gun was loaded and whether the safety was on. He knew a little about guns, as Mike and he would go shooting sometimes when they visited Mike's parents in the countryside. So it wasn't that he didn't appreciate that it was a gun. Or what it might be used for.

It was just a literalness. A customer had asked him to deliver a package. He had never been told to refuse a package before. The rule was only that the base station had to be contacted – the supervisor would check that the rider had time to make the delivery and the package was logged. This was done. And so there was no reason for Randall not to take the package. There was an interpretation of the situation available in which it was perfectly fine to deliver a package containing a gun and Randall took that interpretation – it was the simplest and the one that fitted most swiftly into how he operated as a bicycle courier.

After the film finished, Randall and Mike remained seated in the front row. We watched through to the end of the credits and still they remained seated. Then Mike stood up and surveyed the empty theater.

'So, this is what we do,' he explained. And he and Randall jumped over the seats in the front row. And then the next row. And the next. They were both laughing and clearly racing each other. I gave chase, watching their hurdling technique and trying not to lose further ground. Mike won easily, Randall came second, and I dragged in last. They both offered their palms to me for high-fives. We stood panting, looking down at the empty cinema, the seats stretching out below us like fungi.

'Ready?' asked Randall.

I lost again. Randall grabbed Mike's left foot about half-way down and prised off his shoe. Mike shouted at him but his laughter won through. He picked up his shoe and threw it down to the front and continued tumbling over the seats. Randall won and waited for us, beaming, holding up Mike's shoe like a trophy.

On our way out of the complex, Randall switched on his cell phone. He held it out to Mike, who checked his messages.

'Hey, did you give this gun guy your phone number?' asked Mike.

'He wanted to check when the package got delivered,' replied Randall.

'And that was last thing today?'

Randall nodded. Mike shook his head and chuckled.

'See, there's two more guys wanting you to deliver packages for them. And they're saying "packages" in a special way, like it's a code word. Do you know what that's about?'

Randall sat down on a bench. He placed the palms of his hands on his knees and focussed his gaze on a spot between his feet.

'Fucking hell. Randall's going to be a gun-runner,' Mike exclaimed. He turned to me in an interrogative way – why wasn't I laughing? I was watching Randall. He was very still.

'Will you call them please, Mike, and tell them to call the office?' he asked. Mike nodded, of course, of course, and began to do so. I sat down next to Randall and asked him if he needed anything. He paused and then asked me please not to sit next to him. I stood. Mike came over with the phone.

'Will you call the second one?' he asked me. 'Wait, I'm just connecting.' He walked away again. The call didn't last very long. 'OK, fine. Hey, will you call the second one? I think it'll be funny when this guy gets a British accent on the phone. What do you think, Randall?'

Randall looked up and nodded. I shrugged and took the

phone from Mike. It was already ringing. I closed my eyes and focussed on tapping my left foot. I wasn't good at phone calls. I avoided them as much as possible; I found them difficult as I couldn't see the other person's reaction and I worried that I wouldn't be able to work out enough information from the other person's tone of voice. I sent emails; at work, I went and saw people at their desks instead; I often let the phone at home ring out then checked the number and rang the caller back – this meant that at least I knew who I'd be talking to before I began.

The call went through to voicemail. I left a brief message, and hung up. Mike was moving his hand very slowly towards Randall's head.

'It's OK, baby, it's OK,' he said softly. His hand reached Randall's head and he began to run his hand through Randall's hair, in smooth, circular motions, murmuring from time to time – something indistinct. After a couple of minutes, Randall got up and they hugged. Mike winked at me over Randall's shoulder. When they broke off, he added, 'Let's go home.'

*

When I arrived, Randall and Mike were in the midst of their Frenchification. Every time, before they went abroad, they used this intensive language acquisition technique. They turned all the menus on their appliances to the language of the country that they were visiting – their cell phones, the television, the DVD player. They bought newspapers and magazines from that country and kept them around the house. They stuck Post-it notes on all their household items. Mike talked me through their method as he showed me around their house the next day. It was certainly thorough.

Every piece of furniture was labeled, all the ornaments in the cabinet next to their dining table, even many of the toiletries in their en-suite bathroom. They had done German and Spanish and now, with a trip to Nice planned, they were learning French.

Except it wasn't really learning. The focus of the exercise was the recognition of common terms. Randall sometimes did a little better – he picked up some grammar – but Mike set out, very frankly, that for him it was about knowing the French word for towel so that when you're in your hotel room and the maid is trying to talk to you, you can pick out the word 'towel' and, from her gestures or the context, guess the remainder.

'What is the French word for towel?' I asked, as Mike and I stood in the third of seven bathrooms. It was a huge house. The main staircase was large enough to stage a scene from a spy thriller. The dining table really needed a whole hog on a silver platter at its center to complete the effect.

'Actually, towels are tough,' shrugged Mike. 'It's hard to stick a label on a towel. That's a bad example.'

'Does it work for Randall?' I asked.

'He's extraordinarily good at picking up the words. Usually, he gets the words and I try to do the rest. It's a good partnership. It's how relationships are, aren't they?'

I nodded. Kept nodding. I felt that Mike expected me to think that their relationship was suspect. He knew that I had spoken to Randall's parents. And they weren't convinced – not that their son was gay and not that he ought to be in a relationship.

Randall and Mike had been together since 2000. They met when Mike was working a summer at his father's construction firm and Randall was delivering packages. It was Randall's first relationship, and Mike's too. They moved in together after six months.

Autistic people typically aren't good at relationships. There are communication difficulties. Relationships are complex, not susceptible to rule-governance or local coherence. But the barriers can be simpler than that too. Many autistic people shrink from being touched by others. They can't stand it. They find it overwhelming. I threw temper tantrums for a couple of years when I was a kid. If my parents tried to calm me by hugging me, the tantrums got worse. I remember a child that I saw in a park while I was at college. He was silent; he wasn't speaking yet. He was with his mother. It was a sunny day and she wanted to take his shoes off so that he could feel the grass on his feet. But as soon as she did so, he started crying. He clambered on to a bench. She didn't understand at first, she thought he needed convincing and so she took her own shoes off too and showed them to him. She lifted him off the bench and stood him up on the ground again. He took a few steps and then sought her arms to lift him off. She tried to resist him, but he began screaming and she had to acquiesce. He couldn't cope with the new sensation on the soles of his feet. For me, when this happens, it feels like water has been spilt; it feels like trying to soak it up with tissue paper but there's too much of it and the tissue paper becomes mushy, the water continues to spread.

While some autistic people experience this sort of sensory overload, others prefer to be squeezed very tightly. For these people, Temple Grandin – who has written about her autism, and also designs slaughterhouses – pioneered the 'Hug Box'. The box is made of two padded sideboards which are hinged near the bottom to form a V-shape. The user lies down or squats inside the V. There is a lever, which engages an air cylinder, which in turn pushes the sideboards together. The machine provides deep pressure stimulation evenly across the lateral parts of the body. It has been used in a number of schools for autistic children. Students having a bad day get priority access. Some children prefer short bursts. Others stay in for up to half an hour. The Hug Box disturbs me though – I don't like to think of autistic children climbing into this contraption and self-medicating with hugs. It seems unwise to encourage them in seeking en-closure.

The night before, I had seen a different sort of touch though. I had seen Mike stroke Randall's hair. I had seen how they functioned when Randall became agitated about the messages on his phone. Randall was happy to be touched and, most of all, he wanted to be touched by Mike.

We moved on to the next set of rooms. It was odd to think of Randall and Mike sharing a life in a house that was so large. Somehow, it made their relationship seem like an experiment, as if the house was a gift from the producers of a reality television programme and there were hidden cameras everywhere. In fact, Mike had inherited the house from his father's younger brother, Stephen, or Unc Tevey, as he was known. Unc Tevey had committed suicide after finding out that he was adopted. Mike had told me about him on condition that I must not conclude that his uncle was autistic. His uncle was an architect, like Mike's father, and very successful, at a different firm. He lived on his own. He collected photographs of UFOs but was dismissive of them. He built models and tore them down when he was finished. He wrote long essays on philosophy and kept them in a locked drawer. His will contained two instructions: give the house to Mike; burn my stuff.

Unc Tevey found out that he was adopted at a family party. Mike's father said something to him, using his name, and their mother – who had been ageing rapidly since suffering a stroke six months previously – suddenly announced, with no preamble, 'That isn't his name. It's what we called him. No one knew his name.'

Unc Tevey disappeared after that for about three weeks. When he came back, he seemed fine. He didn't talk about where he had been. No letters ever arrived afterwards suggesting that he had gone looking for his birth parents. He returned, he went back to work, he came to family events – and then, four months later, he shot himself, sitting on a park bench late at night.

'He mumbles the English under his breath,' Mike continued. We were standing at the top of the stairs gazing up through the skylights. I wondered if, towards dusk, they created beams of light, leading down into the hallway.

'I'm sorry.'

'When we're abroad, and he hears a word that he knows, he translates it immediately. He mumbles it under his breath.'

'Do you do that?'

Mike turned and looked at me. 'Of course I don't.'

'Why does he do it?'

'He's very quick at it. If he knows a word, it takes him no time to find it.'

Mike jumped. Someone was knocking at the door. He paused for a moment, then went off to answer it. As I stood at the top of the stairs, I realized that Randall's and Mike's eyes were the same colour: gray and blue, recently combined – glistening, almost in motion. They both had no hair on the backs of their hands and long, slender fingers.

When Mike returned, he looked unsettled.

'What is it?' I prompted.

'Yeah, so – there was a guy just at the door. Navy suit. Smart hair. He was looking for Randall. He said, "Tell him a number of people think it was a good job." That's all he said.'

I leant back against the banister. I had been thinking about the gun story.

'Randall knows a little bit about guns, doesn't he?' I said.

'He knows quite a lot.'

'So this was an ordinary gun. So far as he could tell?'

'That's what he said.'

'Why ask him to take it across town? Why not just drive it across town? Why pay to send it there? If it's just an ordinary gun. Which, so far as we know, it is.'

Mike nodded slowly. Then he turned and started running down the stairs. 'Fucking bastards,' he shouted. He flung open the door and shouted it again. But the man had left already. I caught up with him as he slammed the door. 'Total fucking bastards.'

'It's just really fucking mean,' I replied. We had reached the same conclusion – that these men were messing around with Randall. They wanted to see what happened, where it led. It was the equivalent of sending the new worker down to the storeroom to look for an imaginary stock item, asking the unpopular girl for a date and not turning up. Mike rubbed his forehead and eased back his blond curls, which regularly tumbled down over his eyes.

'I should have realized. I should have realized. It's happened before. There've been receptionists who buy him gifts, lead him into empty offices and test him out. When he came out, there was a guy who kept making insinuations, smacking his lips at him, really fucking mature stuff, you know, and Randall stopped going into this guy's office. He'd stand outside and ring the bell.'

We both stood and shook our heads.

'I'm going to call his office and let them know.' Mike took his phone out of his pocket and headed off to do so.

As I watched him walk away, I thought about when I first began exploring whether this book was feasible. I spoke to my parents about it. I explained that I wasn't in touch with anyone really. We had all been too young when we went to the same school. Would it be possible to retrieve people? My father had laughed and fetched an old address book. There was a page, with old details crossed off many times, slips of paper inserted around it, providing a list of all the parents of my classmates. The parents had kept in touch. We, the students, hadn't.

The parents had kept in touch because they shared the same anxieties. So they monitored the progress of each other's worries. They knew that their children struggled, and that their incapacities were continuing ones. There was unlikely to be a shining day when everything became fine. What did that feel like? To have created a life that was so fundamentally different from their own. Not different interests, a different view about the importance of religion, a partner that you didn't necessarily approve of, but a different sort of life, a person who simply couldn't do some of the things that you could. A person whom you needed to protect until you physically couldn't any more. And who would do it then? Randall's mother had told me about the moment, at the wedding of a friend's daughter, when she had realized that her son probably would never be able to live with someone else, that her son wouldn't go through these stages of life.

But then he did. He met Mike. Mike started appearing at the house, chatting politely, before taking Randall off to a film or out for a meal. Randall started staying away overnight. And then, when Unc Tevey's will was executed, Mike asked Randall's parents to come and look at the house. Randall's parents were affluent, doing just fine, but they weren't rich. They didn't go regularly to houses like the one I was standing in. Their son was supposed to stay with them, in the same room that had been his since he was twelve, not in a house like this. It wasn't a disaster – clearly, it wasn't – but it was an adjustment. Suddenly their son was an adult, a part of another family, and they weren't convinced that he was able to do it. He had never been in a relationship, though he had kissed girls before and, more recently, he had kissed boys. They knew about that. Sometimes from neighbors, or friends, who felt that they needed to pass on what they had seen, as if Randall was a maiden to whose honor they owed their vigilance. But he had never lived away from home before. He even struggled with guests in the house sometimes. They disrupted his routines.

It was working though, mostly. During the year that Randall and Mike had lived together, Randall had left a couple of times. He never explained why. He just arrived, back at his parents' home, without any belongings or clothes. They never pressed him. He slept in his room for a few nights. Mike came around, he went in there, and they spoke at length. And a couple of nights later, on both occasions, Randall moved back out.

His parents wanted him to be well. But they worried. As I waited for Mike to return, I felt almost as if I was compiling a report in my head to deliver to them. I wanted already, and dearly, to phone them and tell them to stop worrying – really, to cease worrying. This was as good as it got. Their son was loved.

*

It began with parallel play. From Randall's perspective, the process by which he came to be in a relationship with Mike began with parallel play.

Autistic children prefer to play on their own, though it's not an informed preference. They prefer to play on their own because they don't understand that it may be possible to play together with another child. When we first started going to our school in New York, we noticed the assorted toys but showed no interest in each other. We didn't peer over each other's shoulders. We didn't ask each other questions. We didn't compare lunchboxes. Our teachers' remedial techniques were, in a sense, rudimentary. They tried to get two of us interested, for example, in the same set of blocks. If one of us started putting all the red blocks together, some of the remaining red blocks were moved to the other child's pile. The red-assembler would then need to negotiate his or her way into the other child's pile in order to retrieve the remaining red blocks, thereby interacting with another mind.

The challenge for autistic individuals is that they are overwhelmed even by their own minds. Typically they notice more details than other people. I know someone who can sketch buildings in architectural detail, from memory – placing not just the rooms but lift shafts, corridors, stairwells – after walking around them only once. Elizabeth, who was in our class and whom I will write about later in the book, could play a piece of music straight through immediately after hearing it for the first time. There is a high incidence of synesthesia too, that is, minds that correlate certain sounds, tastes, or textures with colors. Simultaneously, the ability of autistic individuals to categorize or process this information is more limited. Their language skills are less developed. They don't know how to invoke the assistance of others. With this combination of high input and low output, inevitably a sort of logjam occurs – there is a lot that lingers. Consequently, autistic individuals try to focus on simple tasks, and tasks that don't involve other people. In this way, they begin to manage the throughput of sense data.

As managing our own minds was such a challenge, it was unsurprising that we weren't curious about one another. We had enough going on. Simple, solitary tasks were quite stimulating enough. Not exploring each other's worlds, playing on our own, was part of a containment strategy. Unconsciously so, for we were too young to have thought it through, but it was pragmatic, prescient, pessimistic – it was as if we knew our limits and were reconciled to them.

However, no one else was – not our parents and not our teachers. So they started us off with parallel play. They stole our red bricks and put another child, another mind, between them and us. Obviously we complained. We didn't take to this quickly. Rather than trying to coax the red bricks from the other child, my first tactic was to push the other child out of the way, as hard as I could. I developed a reputation for it. Some of the other parents spoke to my parents about it. The teachers had to convene a conference and explain that they would always be there to keep it in hand but some of this was necessary. Some knee-grazing would occur. Their children would have to make such sacrifices for each other's development. Other children wailed when our games were 'improved'. Sometimes the red-tower project was simply abandoned or frustration was expressed by way of an uncontrolled demolition.

By the time we began listening to Ms. Russell read the newspaper, we had made enormous progress. The school had been open about a year and most of us had been there since soon after the beginning. We sat and listened to her as a group. We understood that we were behaving in the same way as one another. If one person became noisy during the reading, another would complain. We sat close to one another, closer than we strictly needed to sit in order to listen. There remained though an element of otherworldliness about each one of us, a resilient autonomy. We may have been listening to Ms. Russell read the newspaper but we were also keeping to our own activities – drawing on a piece of paper or picking apart a sock using the one loose thread. I traced the outline of the white stripe on the multicolored rug. Craig shouted, 'Send in the Idiots.' But this was progress all the same.

The point from which we had progressed is often described as 'mind-blindness'. There is an emerging orthodoxy among clinicians who work with autistic children that one of the deepest characteristics of autism is the lack of a theory of mind. Autistic children simply don't understand that there are minds other than their own that might have thoughts different from their own. This is why they display so little interest in others. This is why it is so difficult to get them to cohere as a group. The primary evidence for this hegemonic account comes from a series of experiments, of which I will describe one example.

A child is shown a tube of sweets. When asked what is inside the tube, the child replies, 'sweets'. The tube is then opened to reveal no sweets but, instead, a pencil. The lid of the tube is replaced and the child is told that Alex is outside. If Alex was to come in, and he was shown the tube, what would he think is inside it? When this question is asked, non-autistic children tend to give the right answer, which is obviously 'sweets'. Alex is likely to make the same mistake that they did. However, autistic children tend to give the opposite answer. When asked what Alex will think is inside the tube, the child replies, 'a pencil'.

This is used as evidence for the mind-blindness thesis. Autistic children have no conception of other minds and so they assume that Alex will have the same thought that they now do. If it's in their mind, it must be in his too.

I'm sceptical about this explanation. First of all, I doubt whether these experiments are entirely reliable. Autistic children, in particular, are often subjected to a lot of testing. It is possible that the children involved in this experiment are already anxious as a consequence. They may know that they are being tested. And they may know that they have been tested before. They may even have some sense that they have given 'wrong answers' in the past. The first part of the experiment elicits another wrong answer from them. They may be worried about giving yet another wrong answer. They've already been tricked once. Subject to these considerations, are the results from the second stage of the experiment reliable? Are the children's answers affected by 'test anxiety'? Are they trying to second-guess the examiners? After all, the answer that first occurred to them has already been proven to be wrong once. Perhaps they do think of 'sweets' to begin with but change their answer because they don't want to be wrong in the same way again. I'm drawn to this explanation as it suggests that the children involved are smarter, cannier, less passive than the clinicians observing them assume. I was one of those children. I'd like to think better of us. I'd like to think we were winning.

However, I will forgo this partisan explanation, for I believe that there is a more compelling alternative. I am encouraged to think so because of three things: not all the autistic children reply: 'a pencil', my classmates and I learned to sit together as a group relatively quickly; and Randall, still authentically autistic in many other ways, is in a relationship with Mike.

The alternative is this: autistic children aren't unique in lacking a theory of mind. *Everyone* lacks a theory of mind to begin with; it is not something innate. Three-year-olds usually answer 'pencil' too; it is only older children who regularly perform well on such tests. Anyone who has played hide-and-seek with a young child will know that children think hide-and-seek is quite an easy game. If they cover up their eyes, or stick their head behind a sofa, children of two or three years of age think that, as they can't see you, you can't see them either. They assume that your mind is the same as theirs.

Everyone needs to learn how to read other minds. And autistic children – because they develop language later, more slowly, because their own minds are so difficult to manage – they don't learn as quickly or as well as others and need more help in doing so. Even when they have it, their abilities may not be as well-honed as others; because they learnt it later, more slowly, they feel less sure of what they learnt than others; and, as their minds continue to fill so quickly, and the differential between input and output capacity remains – think of a person trapped in a room that is filling with water – sometimes still, even as adults, adults who work jobs, adults in relationships, they begin to struggle. They need to sit down, like Randall at the cinema on the first night that I was there, or flee, like André, when someone interrupted one of his puppets, and focus on something much, much simpler until they can manage again.

I remember learning about indicator lights on cars. One of our neighbors had taken me for a walk; this was when we still lived in New York. It was the middle of the day and there was a lot of traffic. But my neighbor knew when a car was going to turn and when it wasn't going to. I wanted to wait until the 'Walk' sign came on each time, but sometimes, even when there were cars nearby, she knew that we could cross. I asked her about it eventually. And so we sat on a bench along Central Park West and she explained indicator lights to me. Suddenly I could read, almost as well as her, the minds of New York drivers.

All mind-reading takes this form. We learn to look for certain indicators and we learn their effects. We don't know that someone is in pain or anguish. But we can infer their state of mind from expressions or gestures. Some people are better at making these inferences than others. And some-times all of us make mistakes about what is in another person's mind. Actors rely on us doing so. So do liars, spies, and salespeople.

Looking back on it, this was the major premise in the proposition that our school was running. They didn't believe that we lacked the ability to understand the possibility or content of other minds, only that we needed to develop it, like all children do, and that, for us, that process was going to be harder, deliver later results, and we were going to require more guidance.

It began with parallel play. The next step was getting us to talk about other people's feelings. Sometimes in a group, sometimes individually, our teachers played us tapes of two characters, Tom and Maureen, having a discussion. I've gone through the tapes more recently and Tom and Maureen are fairly dull though, at the time, they seemed mysterious. Tom and Maureen spoke about their daughter, who lived far away and didn't visit very often. They spoke about their grand-children, who were messy. Tom's shed needed mending. Maureen broke her favourite chair. These tapes were played, and we were asked to identify how Tom and Maureen might be feeling. We were asked to concentrate on expres-sions and inflections, key words and giveaway phrases.

Since then, the learning tools have become more sys-tematic and elaborate than simple audio tapes. There are computer programs that display facial expressions on an ordinal scale. There are sets of cards for regular practice, in the car, in the park, on the way to school.

The final stage, for us, was talking to a therapist. Even after we left the school, the school provided our parents with contact details for therapists. This was crucial to developing our emotional articulacy. Most children talk to one another about mental states. We didn't so much. And so we needed to talk to adults. We didn't do it easily and so it needed to be structured, an appointment placed in our calendars, a gentle measure of coercion applied.

Developmental psychologists tend to believe that inter-kid conversations are especially important to the development of theory of mind and what lies beyond. Between the ages of two and four, there tends to be a dramatic increase, at least for children without siblings close to their age, in the amount of contact that they have with other children. Those are the crucial years for overcoming mind-blindness. Talking to other children may be particularly effective, as children are more likely than adults to join them in make-believe activities. Those activities rely on taking and talking about other states of mind. It's also that adults tend to compensate for a child's lack of conversational ability. They finish sentences for children and guess at their meaning, rather than asking for a better version. Children are less likely to do that with one another and so communication is more challenging and forces more explicit consideration of others' knowledge and beliefs.

We didn't have these conversations, though. We spoke to adults instead – adults who were trained in not making the same mistakes that other adults do when they talk to children, adults who pressed us for explanations. And, by parts – because we were polite, clever, aware that our parents thought it was important – we tried to provide explanations. In this way, over the course of several years, long after we had left the school, we and our parents adhered to the school's fundamental belief that we could be taught how to read others' minds, even our own.

*

'I think that these are people who occupy a different plane of existence than I do,' explained Mike, as we sat on a park bench – Mike and I, with our eyes open; Randall, with his closed. We had come into town to have coffee with Randall during his break and he had led us into the park. We were talking about organizations that provided support and guidance to the relatives or partners of autistic people. Meanwhile, Randall was trying to prove that so long as the two people walking in from North and South respectively didn't deviate from their line of travel, stop, or encounter an obstacle, he could pinpoint the exact moment at which they would cross.

'The important thing for them about living with an autistic person is that he likes to make models,' Mike continued, 'or that he'll eat half his dessert, then drink his coffee, then finish the dessert, and he won't have it any other way. That he likes coffee up to a certain point in the mug, and it's always the same mug, and he never takes any more or any less than three lumps of sugar and he has to put the sugar in his coffee using these special sugar tongs that his sister bought for him.' The thought flashed through my mind that Randall didn't have a sister or any siblings at all. His eyes were still closed. 'This is important? This is what they talk about. Go to any of these websites or meetings and this is what they talk about.'

By this stage, Mike was holding up his hands in exasperation.

'I can understand that it might be easier to talk about these things. And, you know, it's possible that these groups are a sort of genre. That talking about these things is one of the requirements of the genre.'

Mike was writing a novel. After applying a lot of thought to the issue, he had decided not to train as an architect, like his father and uncle. Mostly, he was at home. He often took a lunch in to Randall. He cooked dinner. There were days when, on his own account, the only other thing he did was peel an orange and swim a length of the heated pool in the basement. More and more though, he spent his days working on his novel. And he was thinking a lot about genre.

'Genre is a pretty powerful concept. But the problem is that there's nothing remarkable about only having your coffee up to a certain point in the mug and, if it's any more than that, you have to take the mug to the sink and spill the rest. That's easy. That's no trouble at all. What you need to be talking about, if you want to talk about your relationship to strangers at all, is what happens when the sugar tongs break. What happens when you break them accidentally? Do you go out and try to find an identical pair? Do you describe that adventure to the group? Or do you tell your autistic partner? Do you say, "Yeah, see the tongs, I broke those"? That's what these people should want to know from one another.'

Randall was silent, as he had been during Mike's entire exposition. The conversation had turned this way when Randall suggested that Mike didn't like to acknowledge that living with an autistic person could be difficult. Mike, it seemed, was trying to deny that this was his view. Randall's eyes were still closed. The two people that he was tracking from behind his closed eyes were now a few footsteps away from one another. Randall raised his hand in a fist and then opened it.

'Now. By the little sign on the railings that says "Toilets" and there's an arrow pointing right. There's a bed of flowers too but it's empty. I think the boy carrying the skateboard under his arm has gone past the woman. He was behind her before but he's now ahead of her. He's perhaps ten meters ahead of her. She was peeling a sweet but she's done that now and she's chewing it.' He opened his eyes and looked first at Mike and then at me. Every element of his predictive account was accurate.

'Where do you perform?' I said. 'I want tickets.'

He smiled and slipped his hand into mine. I didn't know what to do, so I squeezed his hand and he squeezed back. Ten seconds later, he withdrew it.

Later that afternoon, Mike and I waited for Randall outside his office. He was due to finish work soon, but it was difficult to tell exactly when – he helped with invoicing and the auditing of records and was often the last to leave – so we ordered coffee in a place nearby. Mike struck me as the sort of person who always handled these things, decided which place to go to; he always paid. He took a sip and began talking about his book, which wasn't going very well, at least as he told it. 'Sometimes,' he explained, 'I have to ride on trains with my laptop and write down other people's conversations. It's depressing.'

I drank my coffee quickly and pushed my cup away. I was finding it difficult to speak to Randall when Mike was around, which was all the time. It wasn't that Randall didn't speak at all. It was that Mike was a stronger personality than both he and I, so Mike usually ran the conversations. 'Sometimes I even go into my father's construction offices and read their project evaluations. I write out bits of them and see if they do anything to my head while I'm writing them out.'

Suddenly I realized that Randall had arrived, and was facing Mike. He hadn't sat down yet. 'Do you write?' I asked him. Randall didn't realize immediately that I was talking to him. He gradually lifted his gaze. He nodded.

'Randall writes amazing poems; he writes hundreds,' Mike interjected.

'I write poems,' replied Randall firmly as he took a chair. After a moment's pause, he added, 'They're sort of made up of scraps of things. But I like to use formal structures. I like both kinds of sonnets, for example.'

'They're extraordinary,' Mike added. 'Extraordinary.'

That evening, Randall came downstairs, an hour after he had gone up to bed, with three of his poems in a plastic sleeve. I was sitting on the sofa watching television. Mike had gone off to work shortly after Randall had left for bed. I was surprised to see Randall as Mike had told me that he was usually very strict about his bedtime, especially considering he needed to get up so early for work. I switched off the television as Randall sat down next to me. Randall shook his head. He took the remote control from the table and switched the television back on again. He increased the volume three steps and then handed me the plastic sleeve. I was about to remove the pieces of paper, but he stopped me.

'Read them later,' he suggested. 'Send me an email about them. I'd like to know what you think.' He spoke softly and I realized that he didn't want Mike to know that he had come back downstairs.

'What does Mike think?' I asked.

'I don't think that Mike can be objective about them,'

Randall smiled. 'His own writing isn't going well, so he thinks that mine is brilliant.'

I nodded, vaguely. I was distracted by the quality of Randall's insight. I realized that Randall and I weren't supposed to be able to understand others' attitudes with such clarity. I said so and Randall traced figures of eight on the back of his left hand thoughtfully.

'I'd better go back to bed,' he replied. 'Will you come and meet me for lunch tomorrow?'

I nodded.

'Mike's over at his mother's house to have lunch with her and his aunts.'

I nodded again. I wanted to say more things but I didn't want to keep Randall from going to bed. He gave me a hug and slipped away.

After he left, the first thought to come into my mind was of a friend who died in a car crash in 2000. The night before his funeral, with his friends and family gathered, I told the story of the book signing when he freaked out an author by reciting from memory the opening chapter of her book. Others recounted picking books out from his shelves and stating a page number. He recalled not only the text on that page but any marginalia or marks. He was well-known for locking himself away for days at a time to finish a piece of work. He was also well-known for being manipulative of his friends. He possessed incredible charisma and he set his friends challenges to test their allegiance to him. He attempted to steal away girlfriends and boyfriends, just because he knew he might be able to. He was often intensely cruel about any piece of work or any opinion that you happened to share with him.

At his funeral, he became a 'genius'. His aunt gave the eulogy and, some way through, she pronounced him a genius. This term got picked up for the remainder of the day and it has remained in currency. Many of his family and many of his friends are prepared to declare, quite straight-forwardly, that he was a genius and we must not talk about the other things. Some of us though are left rubbing our foreheads and thinking, no. No, that is not quite right.

But it is understandable. The term obscures, it provides an area of grace. The problem with the term 'genius', however, is that we do not only use it for the purposes of bereavement. We use it commonly. And we use words and attitudes that are similar in effect. I thought of this friend after Randall left, for it seemed to me that Mike was doing something similar with Randall.

When Mike referred to Randall's poems, when he spoke of him reverentially, it seemed to me that he was trying to elevate Randall, or at least set him apart; in a way that is odd for a lover, to refuse to engage with all of him. When we call someone a genius, or special, or extraordinary, we mean that they are blessed with a natural faculty that we are not. They are different from us. We cannot understand what it is like to be them. We must excuse them certain flaws and certain eccentricities – these are necessary corollaries of the great gift, ways of dealing with the burden that is borne. Did Randall's autism put him in this same category as far as Mike was concerned?

Ray Monk's biography of Ludwig Wittgenstein provides an example of this attitude. Monk is fairly frank about Wittgenstein's character. Wittgenstein was incredibly self-absorbed. He could be fantastically rude (don't brandish pokers at visiting lecturers, Karl Popper may or may not have once chided him). He could be cruel. He would tell lesser students (and lesser academics) that they really ought to give up on philosophy. As Monk relates, he physically beat the school students that he taught in Austria. We also know that Wittgenstein had sexual relationships with one or more of his students. Usually we mind when academics do this. We believe that they are abusing a position of power and trust. However, Monk is prepared to forgive Wittgenstein for everything. His book is even subtitled 'The Duty of Genius'. And while I have no interest in doing so, surely an alternative story could be told in which Wittgenstein's self-absorption was due to a sense of self-importance, his treatment of other people indicative of the same. A biographer ought at least to consider these matters. I believe that it is unacceptable to ascribe all of this moraine to the duty of genius.

Monk's biography of Bertrand Russell is quite different. Indeed, Monk confesses that by the end of the process he really didn't like Russell very much. Russell cheated on his wife. He had his son consigned to a mental institution and then refused to see him. However, again, though I am not committed to telling the story this way, it is possible to see Russell as something other than contemptible. For instance, Russell was never anything but clear and blunt with his first wife about the nature of their relationship. She was to be his domestic partner, but he would look elsewhere for lively company and for intellectual fulfillment. She accepted his terms. Russell was to some extent afraid of his son. There was a history of mental illness in the bloodline and Russell had frequent doubts about the extent of his own sanity. I don't want to absolve Russell. But it is crucial to note that

Wittgenstein wins redemption from Monk because he is a genius, and in the critical, though not hostile, account of Russell's life, the word 'genius' is conspicuously absent. Monk applies what we might call full and proper rigor to the life of the ordinary, though very clever, subject but not to the life of the genius.

The term 'genius', when applied to works as part of a lexicon of superlatives including 'masterpiece' and 'one of the finest novels in recent memory', obscures just as much. Though this use of the term brings out a slightly different problem. After all, it is not as if a writer, or artist, or film maker (or inorganic chemist) resolves at the very outset of the creative process to make a work of genius. *In the beginning was the Word. And the Word was Genius.* If the task of criticism is somehow to explain, or make guesses, or lead interesting speculations as to how works come to be or how they do what they do, the use of the term 'genius' must be eschewed. It reveals nothing, it gives no insight into the creative process; by using it, we get no further.

Sometimes our use of the term 'genius' implies that we believe that there is a group of people with some fantastic natural capability to produce thoughts or objects out of thin air. Bobby Fischer, the chess player, is commonly repre- sented – or used to be represented, when his fame was somewhat greater – as an unworldly genius. Here was a working-class boy from Brooklyn who suddenly emerged into world-championship-level chess. He refused to employ standard openings. He played aggressively, unconvention- ally; no one could devise a strategy to contain him. During an adjournment, when his opponents would rush off to find a chessboard to continue their analyses, Fischer would relax and goof off. When we focus on these aspects of the Bobby Fischer legend, however, in some way we actually belittle his achievement. We make it seem as if he had nothing really to do with it, as if it was all very easy and a bit of a laugh. And yet, for many years of his life, Fischer spent up to fourteen hours a day studying chess. The ten years before the world championship match that he won were spent with a chessboard by the bedside and stacks of chess books in every room. Similarly, Wittgenstein produced two extraordinary works of philosophy, but those works were the products of long, hard, sometimes disillusioning, years of thought and study. Wittgenstein was known to weary even Russell, a man who wrote an average of two thousand words a day over the span of his ninety-eight-year life. The friend that I brought up earlier had to lock himself away devotedly for long periods of time to produce his brilliant essays. Genius has to work hard too. Our conception of the privileges of genius is a false one.

I wonder also if our reliance on this term betrays a flawed view of how progress occurs. If most people were asked to explain, for instance, the development of modern physics, they would name particular individuals. No doubt they would pause and describe many of these individuals as geniuses. They probably would not name particular universities, or groups of thinkers, or exchanges of letters. They would miss the importance of shared experience, or discussion, or mutual assistance.

The term 'genius' may be one element of our broader view in which progress relies on a series of daring leaps made by great individual minds. However, this view neglects to consider how it is that great individual minds come to the point at which they can make a leap and the extent to which other people and institutions are involved in that.

Fischer, for example, studied chess books avidly, studied from a very young age the games played by those before him. Wittgenstein needed Russell, as well as the stimulation of the Cambridge environment, the prompts of previous works of philosophy, correspondences with other philosophers. Modern physics relied for its development on the emergence of a culture that valued a particular kind of learning and on the fading of a fundamentally different view of the world. Modern physicists contributed to the eventual demise of that view, but they also relied on it.

Genius too has to engage with a tradition. Genius relies on a social and intellectual backdrop. Without this universe of others, genius would be able to contribute nothing. There would just be sound and fury. Yet, in our view of these things, we seem only to ascribe value to, to admire and remember and venerate, the individual, not what was there before nor what lay beneath. This is an autistic view of intellectual and social progress, one focussed on the role of the *autos*.

Perhaps, though, the greatest achievement and the finest use of the term 'genius' is that it makes us feel safe. By using this term, we identify a group of individuals who are different from us and we refuse to engage with how it is that these individuals do what they do. We accept that their achievements are beyond our ken. We even suggest that their achievements do not depend on anything but the special quality of genius itself. Genius doesn't rely on us. Genius just is. Hence the overall effect is that we completely rid ourselves of any responsibility for progress. We don't have to understand what they do. We don't have to aspire to do it ourselves. In return, we give the geniuses certain special privileges. We cannot hold them to ordinary standards of behaviour, for example. And, in the end, we are able to remove ourselves from the great game. This is incredibly liberating. We can now enjoy our private lives. We need never feel anxious about our 'contribution'.

I can't claim that Mike's outlook was as broad as this. I don't want to. That would be unfair. But it's worth identifying this view for, as I sat on the sofa, watching basketball, with both of my hosts in separate rooms upstairs, I felt that there was something similar at play in how Mike related to Randall.

Of course, he loved him very much. Of course, he wanted to and did care for him. My gloss was that, implicated in Mike's concern was a sense that Randall was special and remarkable, different from himself. This was a good thing because it meant that Mike was always responsive to Randall's distinctive needs. This was also a useful thing because it meant that Randall's abilities posed no threat and no challenge to Mike's own.

Randall wrote amazing poems. But this was because he was autistic. The poems derived from that uncommon feature of his mind. By believing this, Mike was able to continue writing himself, to not be intimidated by the quality of Randall's writing. However, though this part of it was understandable, perhaps even a necessary tactic of self-defense, Mike's attitude also diminished the significance of Randall's writing. It meant that Randall's writing flowed purely from his autism. That it required no graft, no technique, no agonizing – it just emerged. And that wasn't fair. And that wasn't accurate. As I read Randall's poems, I realized not only that they were really good but that they were worked-on, like all good art is. Creative activity is hard work. This is true for geniuses. It is true for Mike and, equally, for Randall.

I stayed on the sofa for a long time that night. Mike joined me after a couple of hours.

'Good night?' I asked.

'Really good,' he replied with a smile. I kept my peace. He got us drinks from the kitchen and we watched some more sports.

*

When I arrived at Randall's office the next day, he still wasn't back from his morning round. I left and spent some time standing in the lobbies of big buildings. I liked doing so. I liked standing, with my hands in the pockets of my coat, looking around periodically as if I was waiting for someone, and then suddenly stalking off, departing with a flourish. I had started doing this as a child when I stayed in hotels with my parents. I often came down to breakfast before my parents or ordered a juice in the café later in the day and drank it on my own. I became conscious that this made me seem interesting; people often asked me who I was and what I was doing downstairs alone.

On my way back to Randall's office, I bought sandwiches, drinks, and pastries. All the cafés nearby seemed to be very busy and I thought that there may be somewhere inside where we could sit and chat more easily, so I went in to the reception desk. Randall had just got back and he was delighted to see the bag in my hand. He led me out, through the back, into a courtyard so small that it might have existed only because the architects of the buildings around it had rounded down some of their measurements. Randall preferred a different account. He liked to think that the buildings surrounding it were moving slowly apart, like on tectonic plates, and that the courtyard hadn't existed at all until a few years ago.

Randall's supervisor kept two chairs there. It was where he and Randall often drank their coffee in the mornings. I sat down on the wrong seat – the one that Randall was used to – but Randall insisted that this was fine. I hadn't noticed such demarcations in the house; perhaps it was his manager who insisted that they keep the same seats each time they sat there. The courtyard was quiet, though you could listen for the sounds of traffic. Sitting there, it felt like they were emanating from the sky, perhaps from birds circling overhead.

Randall ate very carefully. He spread a napkin over his legs and picked any crumbs from it after each bite. I told him that I had read his poems. They were surprising, but they shouldn't have been. I had read them as if they were the poems of an autistic person, and I shouldn't have. The meter was perfect, but that's the nature of sonnets. I didn't want to patronize him and kept worrying, with each statement, that this was exactly what I was doing.

Randall stopped me. 'Mike sent a bunch of them off to an autism website a while ago. That annoyed me.'

I nodded. I didn't want to be right about this. I didn't want Mike to have worked Randall's autism into a fine and delicate mesh. Randall knew what I was thinking; he feared it too. What was he supposed to do? He did need special care. Mike did need to watch out for things. Mike needed to treat him like an autistic person. But Mike also needed not to treat him that way. Randall didn't want to push Mike away, because Mike was helpful, because Mike was kind. Yet, sometimes, he was going to be justified in doing so.

Randall wiped a tear away from his eye. I didn't know what to say and I didn't know what to do. I didn't like this role. André's sister, Amanda, had sent me a text message just a couple of days before: 'You shine a light. You may not mean to, but you do.' I didn't call her back to find out what she meant. I didn't want to extricate Randall's feelings of resentment or frustration towards his partner from behind the carapace that he had adopted. I wanted to pass through the lives of my former classmates without tampering, without changing anything, not even accidentally trampling on a butterfly – just making a few notes, having a few conversations, and then leaving. Now Randall was crying and it wasn't working out that way. I suddenly realized that I had expected to write only about my classmates, not about the people around them; my conception of this book had itself been an autistic one and it couldn't be sustained.

I put down my sandwich and went over to him. I tried to put an arm around his shoulder. He shrugged it away.

'I need you not to do that,' he said, in a flat tone. I was reminded of my first night there when he got upset at the cinema and didn't want me to sit next to him. I was reminded of Temple Grandin's 'Hug Box' – the intolerance that autistic people demonstrate towards some grades of touch and their craving for others. I went back to my own seat. It was Mike who knew how to fix this, not me.

We sat in silence for about five minutes. Then Randall began to speak again. His voice was better. He took a drink.

'Mike has slept with other people,' he began. 'I think he's sleeping with someone else even now.' I shook my head involuntarily. Randall didn't notice. This news didn't cohere with the account that I was developing. Or did it? Perhaps it was possible that Mike, having adopted the position of a carer, felt that fulfilling those responsibilities thoroughly released him from others. Randall looked up. 'Did anyone come to the house during the day?'

I thought for a moment and shook my head. The only time that I even remembered the doorbell going off was when the man in the suit had come to continue the game with the gun. Had Mike looked startled before he went to answer the door? Did he expect that it was someone else at the door and that a disloyalty on his part was about to be revealed? I didn't know. I hadn't noticed anything particular at the time.

'It happened twice quite early on,' Randall continued. I felt as if he had said these words to himself many times, that he had practiced them but that they might come out differently anyway. 'After we moved in together. When I found out about it, I left. I was too angry and too sad. But he came and got me both times. He talked to me. He held my face in his hands. I never told him that I knew.'

I reached over with my handkerchief to stop Randall from using the napkin that he had draped over his legs to wipe his eyes. Did Randall's parents know some of this? Was this why they had told me, albeit in a reticent way, that they 'just weren't sure'? But I doubted that Randall said these things to many people. I wasn't sure that he would say them to his parents. It was possible that he was saying them for the first time to me. He wasn't blurting them out. He asked me to come and see him for lunch. He came downstairs, the night before, after lying in bed for an hour, to ask me to come and see him away from home and away from Mike.

I thought of red blocks as I sat waiting for Randall to continue speaking. I was pretty sure that he didn't want me to start making replies. At least not yet. I thought of red blocks – such a childish image – in the setting of our school, in the main room, and of Mike having taken some of Randall's red blocks and now Randall didn't have all the blocks that he needed.

I wanted him to talk faster, with fewer pauses. I knew that he needed to leave for his afternoon round soon. Patiently, he picked up his sandwich and took another bite. Still holding the sandwich in one hand, he cleared crumbs from his lap with the other. I felt a raindrop fall on my head. But it wasn't followed by another. I looked up and the jagged piece of sky that I could see, past the tops and overhangs of the surrounding buildings, was almost clear. Randall finished his sandwich and picked a grape off the top of his fruit tart. As he held it, before his chest, perhaps working out the order in which to remove the remaining pieces of fruit, I realized that he wasn't going to tell me anything else. He had spoken about his relationship. And I had listened. We were going to leave it exactly like this.

*

I left Chicago the next day. Randall and Mike drove me to the train station. They both gave me a hug. Randall kissed me, gently, on each cheek. I almost kicked Mike as I slipped away from them towards the platform. Just to have done something with what Randall had told me. Just as a warning that he wasn't the only person who cared about Randall. But

I didn't kick him. And I didn't make anonymous phone calls to his cell phone from the train, which was my other idea. Instead, I flicked through a set of photographs that Mike gave me as a gift. They had been taken by Mike's cousin, who was enrolled at photography school. They were all photographs of Randall – some taken from the street while Randall was working, diving between cars or into alleyways on his red bike, some taken at home. I took out a pen and tried to write something on the back of each photograph, a caption or a note. But I couldn't, not immediately. I looked through the photographs until I felt tired, when I put my head down on the table. The plastic cooled my face and I closed my eyes.

I thought of a conversation that I had with a therapist when I was around twelve or thirteen years old. Her name came off the list that the school had provided to my parents. I annoyed her, because I preferred to try and talk about the books on her shelves, and because I pretended that I had friends that I didn't. I also read the magazines in the waiting room and then quoted from them when she asked me questions about how I felt. One afternoon I had just done this, and she recognized the article. She banged her fists down on her desk and shouted at me, 'Kamran, it's OK to be inarticulate, it's OK to be sad.'

I was a mean child though. I started reciting, in a monotone – 'it's OK to be inarticulate, it's OK to be sad' – until she swept out of the office, slamming the door behind her.

Remembering the story made me smile, and it was only when I smiled that I realized I had been crying.

3

'LINES TO TAKE.'

'I'm sorry; what are they?'

'It's a set of lines to take. It's an example that I thought might be useful.'

The interviewer paused. Craig knew what happened next. It was his third interview in as many days. He felt that including a set of lines to take broadened his portfolio. He was sensitive to the need to do so, to make a deeper mark, but it wasn't working.

Craig was a speech-writer primarily, so he included three recent speeches in his application pack – all prepared for US senators. Usually speech-writers worked on the text and that was where their involvement ended. However, Craig was often asked to help with preparing briefings for question and answer sessions that may take place before or after the speech, with journalists or with members of the audience. Some of the answers needed to be charming, some combative; some needed to convey that there was a glint in the speaker's eye; some needed to be something other than an answer while still sounding like one.

It was possible to dismiss speeches as essays, but lines to take were different. It wasn't just a different sort of writing; preparing such briefings required a critical and nuanced understanding of what perspectives the questioners may bring. More importantly, including them in your portfolio, Craig had been told by a colleague, proved that campaign staff trusted you, that they asked you to work with them, share late-night pizzas, talk about threats and opportunities, that you weren't just a brain hired to provide good sentences.

Craig began tapping his right hand on the arm of the chair. It was his third interview in as many days and he knew that the interviewer was about to explain that, while good written communication was vital to the role that he had interviewed for, there was also a strong emphasis on interpersonal skills and practical experience.

Craig wanted to stop him before he began, explain about ordering in food, all the men with their shirtsleeves rolled up, trying out ideas on flip charts – he could be interpersonal. The lines to take document in his portfolio proved it.

Craig wanted to tell him about practical experience. Craig wanted to explain that perhaps he had never made photocopies, and perhaps he had never chaired a meeting, or managed a publication process, but there was the time when he was in Barcelona with a girl who said she liked him. He was trying to like her too so, one night, when she paused outside a designer's window and talked him through the genius of a particular outfit, he noted the name and address of the store. When he got back to Washington, DC, he bought a Spanish grammar and a Spanish dictionary and he sat up till early next morning composing a letter, setting out the date that they had seen the outfit, an account of its brilliance, his address and credit card details. To complete the flourish, he also asked them to send him the mannequin. He picked up the package a week later, brought it to his neighborhood in a taxi, explained the situation to a woman who ran a small boutique nearby, and set it up in her window. He invited the girl around for dinner, took her for a stroll, paused outside the shop window, and, though he had to remind her that it was the outfit she had seen in Barcelona, she gave him a huge hug and was fulsome in her gratitude. It took her three months to explain that she didn't like him enough. But it was practical experience. It showed initiative. And an ability to solve problems creatively.

Now his right foot had begun to tap, too. There was the time when two of his friends had started talking about balancing eggs on their ends at the spring equinox, how the equal duration of night and day and what this meant about the position of the earth relative to the sun's gravitational field made it possible to do so. Plus, they had seen it on television. They expected him to refute the suggestion, but he didn't, because he had an idea. He went out the next day and bought dozens of eggs. He was going to find a way to balance them on their ends. He bought the cables that go with saline drips and tried draining the eggs. He thought about ways to ceramicize the base of the eggs. He refused to research the matter on the Internet. Then, with a day to go, he found a way. He prevailed by sticking tiny strands of paper on to the end of the eggs – tiny, so that they looked like imperfections on the surface of the shell, but arranged so that they stopped the eggs from rocking and then toppling. He prepared a dozen eggs in this way and took them over to his friends. He didn't explain that he had fiddled with the eggs; he just enjoyed their delight at being right about the spring equinox.

Practical problem-solving. Innovation and resilience. He felt that he could make the case. But he didn't say any of these things. The interviewer was already gathering together his papers. He was explaining that theirs was a small policy organization and everyone had to work across the piece, get involved in a range of projects, but that there may be other opportunities in the future – research positions or short-term requirements for writing policy papers or pamphlets.

Craig was tapping both his feet. His right hand was getting louder. He was beginning to introduce a rhythm element through his fingers. It was his third interview in as many days and it was ending in the same way as the previous two. He hadn't worked in two months and he was bored and he wasn't leaving the house enough and he had cut back to buying just three newspapers a day. He was a good speech-writer. He knew that he was. He had a great CV in speech-writing. He had worked for US senators. In the 2004 primaries, he had written for a candidate for the Democratic nomination for president. But he had never held a proper job. And all his referees talked about were his speeches. So every interview was ending in the same way and there wasn't another major election campaign, no rich seam of speeches, for at least another eighteen months.

The interviewer cleared his throat. Craig looked up and made eye contact for the first time. He knew that eye contact could help to build trust and he frequently read terrifying folk statistics, such as 'ninety per cent of communication is non-verbal', but he hadn't yet been able to discipline himself to maintain eye contact effectively. He had to look away within seconds. He could tell from a corner of his gaze that the interviewer was regarding him either sternly or with bemusement. Certainly he had stopped talking. Craig realized that he was now tapping both his feet on the ground and both his hands on the sides of the chair and that he should probably stop and it was probably this behavior that was drawing the look. But he didn't want to stop. He had no urge to stop. He liked the sound that he was making. He was no longer thinking about the interview and the answers that he failed to give. He was watching his hands and his feet and modulating the percussion.

The interviewer stood up.

'Thank you for coming in though. And, like I say, there might be stuff we can collaborate on in the future.'

Craig didn't move. The interviewer shifted nervously on his feet. The beat was building to a crescendo. Craig was concentrating quite hard. He could feel muscles in his thigh begin to twitch, but in a good way. The interviewer tried clearing his throat again. He rested his hand on the telephone receiver, trying to decide what to do next. But then, all of a sudden, Craig stopped. His right hand beat the last note. He went over the peak. He stood, shook the interviewer's hand, and left.

★

Craig was the classmate who introduced the term 'Send in the Idiots' to our sessions with Ms. Russell. It wasn't the only instance of echolalia. His father was a senior executive with a Fortune 500 company and frequently led seminars and made speeches. It was something he took seriously. He'd often walk around the house practicing from flashcards. Craig picked up phrases that his father used and repeated them in our classes. I don't remember these, but Ms. Russell said that her favourite was 'enhanced functionality', that she would laugh every time Craig said 'enhanced functionality', even after several weeks, even though she got looks from the other teachers.

Craig left soon, though, to join a regular class in a school established and run by Jesuits. I didn't meet him again until we were both fifteen. It was in a hotel lobby in New York. My family and I were living in Pakistan by this stage, though it had already been decided that they would move to Glasgow soon and that my higher education, due to start at around the same time, would be either British or American. We were staying in the hotel and Craig and his parents had come to visit us. What I remember vividly is that, as we were crossing the lobby, he knocked over a vase with a trailing arm and I caught it. There was a miniature round of applause from some of the other guests and the hotel staff and that effectively guaranteed that Craig was sore towards me for the rest of the evening. I tried a couple of times to start a conversation between us and our parents tried more frequently but he wasn't having it. I didn't mind too much because I had a magazine with me, so I read that instead, though afterwards my mother explained that he was feeling bad about the vase and that I should have been more self-effacing.

At dinner, one of the conversations that our parents tried to initiate was about college. We had both applied, by chance, to the same liberal arts institution in the Northeast. Though I hadn't yet told my parents, I had already decided that I wasn't going to go there. I had grown up in big cities and this place was in the countryside. The sounds were all different. There was no thum or whirr from the traffic. There was no vague kir-kir of distant voices. There was birdsong and silence instead and I knew that it would bother me. I knew that it would keep me awake. Birdsong was sound with intended meaning, even if that of non-humans; it varied, it fell and rose. I much preferred the steady, inexpressive sound of traffic – I found it calming. Also, it turned out that I wanted to stay at home. I hadn't lived away from home at all. My family had moved a lot and I had moved with them. My parents had never considered leaving me in a school where I was settled or, knowing that their lifestyle would be itinerant, saving me from it by enrolling me in a boarding school. It was only on thinking about college that they first allowed themselves to believe that it might be possible for me to live away from them. I must have decided that this faith was premature; though, as I remember it, I rejected each faraway college for distinct and colossal failings such as being too close to birdsong.

Craig and I didn't meet again until September 2004, in the midst of the US presidential campaign. The candidate that Craig worked for had lost the race for the Democratic nomination and Craig had begun doing other work on a freelance basis as well as going to interviews for full-time positions. We emailed a few times beforehand. We established that, since our last meeting, we had both notched up law and philosophy degrees, me in that order, him in the opposite order. We spooked each other further by discovering that neither of us went to the college that both our parents wanted us to go to – Craig also went to college in his hometown.

We met in New York, on the steps outside Columbia University Library. In our last email exchange we had, for identification purposes, told each other what we were going to be wearing. Craig spotted me first; he called out my name as I climbed up towards him: 'Kamran?' His voice was flat, the same as that of both André and Randall; though he had asked a question, he didn't raise his tone at the end. He was sitting with a senatorial aide. He explained that he was being briefed to prepare a set-piece policy address as part of a memorial event for an eminent judge, and then returned to the conversation.

The aide set out what was needed. The essential theme was crime and punishment. It was a high-profile audience, with lots of key groups represented, and the campaign staff were going to do a lot to generate media interest. The aide stopped talking. Craig tapped his right foot on the stone three times. He had been writing as the aide spoke. He tore off the top page from his notebook and started reading from it steadily.

'Obviously we need two quotations from the judge's opinions or other writings – I'd like one of those quotations . . . You don't need to write this down; may I give you my piece of paper? I'm just reading it now so we can talk about some of this stuff if we need to . . . I'd like one of those quotations to set out three values, or have three parts, some sort of trilaterality, because the speech will be in three sections and I'd like the second quotation I use to give the speech its structure rather than bring a structure in from outside; we need a story, preferably one involving the senator or his father, to do with the judge, some kind of personal connection, and if there isn't one, you need to tell me as soon as possible; we need a second story involving a member of the audience, or an entire constituency, that you really want to touch, and that story has to involve the judge also; please give me all the statistics you'd like to include early on, because otherwise I collect my own statistics and sometimes people don't like me to do that, but tell me if that's OK, because I'd love to do it; if you could also give me effectively a copy of every speech, as delivered, that the senator has given since his election, that would be really helpful and it'll mean that I write, straight off from the first draft, in his voice, or close to it. But before I do that, I'll prepare a page of messages, in accordance with what you've told me here and the papers that you've given me – tomorrow, this will be – and if you could run that through the stops in the campaign office, and with the senator, we'll have a good start and hopefully you'll feel good about the assignment. It's an interesting speech. Thank you very much for hiring me. I'm really grateful.'

Craig tapped his right foot again, three times. The aide looked over at me and smiled.

'What's the senator's position on capital punishment?' I asked her.

'He doesn't want to be drawn on that, but he's a cautious supporter of it. It's a not a big campaign issue for him. His opponent is pretty much in the same place.'

I turned to Craig. 'What if he gets asked?'

Craig shrugged. 'If it's in the context of the event, and if the judge was a cautious supporter too – I think he was – the senator should state his view briefly, and then quote from the judge. If the judge has no helpful writings on the matter, then he should say something around difficult issue, terrible crime, consideration of the victim and victim's family, so when the state has to make a decision about life and death, it's critical it is made by judges of this quality. It needs that ending to help make the question go away. Sensitive to its importance but, like you're saying, it's not a campaign issue, and we don't want to spend extra time on it.'

The aide let out a long, soft whistle. 'Wow,' she exclaimed. 'Would you be happy to come in and help us knock around some Q&A towards the end of the week? This, and some other issues?' she asked quietly.

Craig nodded. 'I'd really like that. Thank you.'

The aide gathered together her things, Craig handed her his note, and she left.

'Hey,' I said, as soon as she was out of earshot.

'Hey,' Craig replied.

And we both sat there and grinned.

*

A couple of days later, we were sitting at the back of an emptying hall in New York University. There were men on the stage taking apart scaffolding on which there had been seats a little while earlier. It looked like they were pulling limbs out of sockets. It was vaguely painful. The hall itself was still throbbing with excitement. President George W. Bush was in New York to address the UN General Assembly and we had just listened to Senator John F. Kerry counter with a major policy speech on Iraq. It was mid-September, the election was around seven weeks away, final terms and conditions for the debates were close to being agreed, and the candidates were beginning to shift up from the long jog of the last six months.

Craig and I had resolved to take a comprehensive interest in the campaign. We were reading multiple newspapers, checking news websites five or six times a day, and we were planning to attend any and all events in New York State. We both expected Senator Kerry to win, but it wasn't just that we were cheerleading for our own side; we had a professional interest too. No one in the Democratic party was talking properly about jobs in a Kerry administration but Craig felt that, if he had a good season doing freelance writing, he was in the running for a communications post. Though I didn't have as direct an interest in the outcome of the campaign, I function in the same sort of world as Craig – I work for the UK Government, preparing advice for ministers as well as writing speeches. Our lives form a too-straightforward double helix, convergence followed by divergence followed by . . . well, this could go on. We started in the same class, when we were tiny; we failed to go to the same college, though for the same reason; now we work the same sort of job.

'He needs to split the war into two phases,' Craig pronounced.

I agreed. 'He needs to get away from the rights and wrongs of getting into the war. He needs to say he has a better plan for winning the peace. He started to do that today. This is good.'

'It should be stronger,' Craig complained. I watched as a man, who wasn't wearing shoes, climbed down the steps by the side of the stage carrying microphones, cables trailing behind him. I watched anxiously, in case he might trip.

'It should be stronger,' Craig repeated. I had missed my cue.

'What's the line?' I managed, as the guy carrying the microphones disappeared through a door.

'The war in Iraq is over. That's what he needs to say.'

'Mission accomplished?' I asked, with surprise.

'He needs to say that the war is over in the sense that the first phase, the traditional warfare part, is over. Now what we're facing is an insurrection,' he continued, grasping his theme. 'President Bush is failing to win the peace and so we're now in a new kind of war and a second phase. We're not fighting Iraq, or Iraqis – we are fighting terrorists. Who have come in from all through the region because President Bush failed to secure the borders. They have all kinds of weapons, because President Bush failed to secure arms caches. He then needs to say that President Bush is trying to fight the new war in the old way and Americans are therefore dying.'

Craig wrote his first full speech for the day of his high school graduation. He was elected valedictorian. He had written parts for debates before, he had written presentations for use in class; most of his essays were better read aloud, he felt, but graduation was his first full-length speech.

He began by mining his father's speech-writing books. He learnt about the ascending tri-colon. The task began to please him, thrill him, sustain him. He learnt about floating opposites. His confidence grew, his inhibitions diminished. He went to bed with a dictionary of quotations and folded the page whenever he spotted one with potential. He began to mutter sections of the speech to himself in the shower, while walking, while lying in bed in the morning waiting for the alarm clock to go off. His father brought home a lectern one night and set it up in the hall for Craig to rehearse the speech properly. Initially, he only used it when everyone else had gone to bed, but on the night before graduation, his family assembled on chairs borrowed from the dining-room and listened to him deliver the entire address. He didn't look up from his text once, even though he knew it all off by heart. His parents took him out to dinner afterwards – they were proud, surprised, apprehensive.

There was obviously never any prospect of Craig delivering the speech himself the next day. He found it difficult enough to speak up in class. He had to concentrate very hard on what he was saying and any distraction or interruption, even someone dropping a pencil or pages fluttering in the draft, led to a long pause; he needed to assimilate that sense data, understand it, before he could return to his original thought. He also lacked the confidence to stand on a stage or to project his voice; he wouldn't look up from the text when he spoke; there was no variation in his tone. No teacher wanted to ask him to speak at graduation and make him feel embarrassed, but they cleared through his parents the idea of getting him to write the speech – he was easily the best essayist in his graduating class. He took to the writing itself with delight. But for him to give the speech at home after completing the writing was a massive and additional achievement and his father breathed a sigh of relief from the anxiety that had been building ever since he ordered the lectern.

On graduation day, his parents' other fears – that he would hate handing the speech over, or make a commotion during the event if the delivery wasn't exactly the same as his own, or that no one would recognize him as the writer – all went unrealized. The speech was a success. His classmate paced a number of sections differently – he pronounced *joie de vivre* and *volenti non fit injuria* as if they were English phrases

– but Craig was dead proud and everyone was very appreciative. People asked for photographs of the speech-giver and Craig, standing side by side.

Craig's career as a speech-writer had begun. His father, for instance, never prepared another set of remarks himself – Craig did them all, even though he started college soon afterwards. He produced a grid of all his father's engagements, conferences, and seminars, put it up on his wall, and never missed a deadline. Some of his father's colleagues started using him too. His performances in the hall became a weekly affair. He saved up the money he was making – everyone, including his father, was strict about paying for his skills – and bought a computer in the second year of college. He started producing final versions using a word processor, for neatness and legibility, ease of use, but he still did most of his writing, and editing, by hand.

His first political speech was for a senator in the State Assembly, the father of a college classmate. He was briefed while lying in hospital recovering from the first and only time he ever got drunk. He was quiet in college. He was barely there. He attended the lectures that he felt were worthwhile and readily disregarded the others. He always picked the same seat in the lecture theatres – end of the row closest to the door – away from the coteries that quickly formed. He usually tried to arrive as late as possible and leave immediately after the end of the lecture. He did the same for seminars. Using his own money and the enthusiasm that his parents had for his studies, he bought all the key texts and so rarely used the library. His assiduous non-intervention in college life nevertheless brought him attention.

From time to time, a girl or a couple of girls would come

and sit next to him, try to walk out with him, suggest lunch. He was tall, with well-cut dark hair and huge, bright eyes – whenever I've spent time with him, I've noticed people look at him, watch him as he goes by, and some of that is because he's good-looking. And, of course, he wasn't withdrawn during college because he was rude or a misanthrope; he wasn't able to talk on the terms that they did and he didn't know the news from around campus because he lived at home. So, whenever the girls or anyone else drew him into a conversation, he asked if they were well, if they had completed the assignment for the class on logic; he asked as many supplementary questions as he could think of: 'It sounds like you had a really bad cold – are you taking some vitamins to build up your system?', 'I don't know the conditions for getting an extension of the deadline – would you like me to find out?' and, when the conversation flagged, he rubbed his brow, issued a 'Good to have met you' or 'I hope you have a good evening', and left.

From time to time, the attention he received was meaner. Someone would accidentally-on-purpose bump into him. Or, meaner still, spill something over him. Or ask him about his girlfriend – or is it boyfriend? His parents had always counseled him strictly that he was to walk away from these situations or, failing that, to sit down on the ground and be utterly passive. His mother had been bullied in school and the latter was her winning strategy. The problem for Craig was that he looked like a worthwhile adversary. He dressed well, he was handsome and, as others saw it, attentive to women. Some bullying, his parents reassured him, was inevitable. He just needed to find ways not to make it escalate. So he'd sit down on the ground whenever he started to feel a little bit panicky, and they'd laugh at him, or circle briefly, but it never lasted long, and it never became too unpleasant.

The boy who invited him to the party was a philosophy classmate and they had worked together on a group assignment. He wasn't autistic, but he was quiet and clever, and Craig expected that there would be dinner around a table, so it was safe to go along and perhaps he could leave shortly afterwards. He didn't like being lonely around campus and this was a manageable opportunity to do something about that – there might be other people who were gentle and easy to get along with.

It turned out, though, to be a more expansive party. There were around a hundred people there when Craig arrived, and a lot of alcohol. Craig drank wine at home with his family but always in moderate quantities. Sometimes he drank a beer with his father on a summery Sunday. He decided to leave the party shortly, but not so shortly as to be completely rude. In the kitchen, he was offered a drink, and that was OK, except that the person who offered it thought it would be really funny to get him drunk and so poured whiskey instead of beer, but in the same quantity as beer. Craig didn't know enough about beer or whiskey to realize what trick had been played, and, as he walked around the crowded house, he kept deciding to leave earlier and earlier, and he drank faster and faster, so that he could finish the cup and leave, until, overwhelmed by the amount of alcohol, he fell down dramatically on the patio.

Both the classmate and his parents spent the night at the hospital with Craig's parents. Craig didn't come to until the morning. A doctor interviewed him thoroughly, shone a light into his eyes, got blood tests back, and everyone breathed a sigh of relief. By the time the senator in the State Assembly, the classmate's father, came in to speak to Craig, he already knew about the excellent college grades and had heard from Craig's father about how much writing Craig had done already, and, though that was obviously a partial account, he decided to commission a brief policy speech. He needed something strong, he could use the research and preparation time to do other things, and, after all, the fall had happened in his house and this would contribute to the amends-making. Craig immediately sat up and asked for a notebook. His mother offered the address book from her handbag and Craig started making notes in the 'XYZ' section.

Once the two men had carried out the lectern, Craig and I were the last people left in the hall. The stage had been completely dismantled. The only remaining mark of the rally was a banner that someone had left on a seat. It read, simply, 'Kerry Edwards 2004'. Craig was showing no signs of wanting to leave and I was running through sections of the speech that Senator Kerry had made in my head. Analyzing policy like this is what I do professionally.

Craig ended up as a speech-writer because he got drunk. My route into my job was a different one. I studied law as an undergraduate, largely because my parents felt that I should have a profession. Perhaps especially for someone like me – who wasn't going to make a million by being entrepreneurial, for whom education had begun as a way out of silence (I didn't speak until I was four and until after I had started at the school in New York), and for whom the experience of then moving through the mainstream education system had been puzzling and stressful – perhaps especially for an autistic person, it was important that college lead to a formal accolade, an obvious qualification. Though I studied law, I quickly decided that I wasn't going to become a lawyer. I had become interested in the philosophy of law instead – questions of law's legitimacy, the proper role of law, its links to morality and social power. Also, everyone else in my class wanted to become a lawyer and it seemed to involve lots of interviews, going to drinks receptions and picking strategically which people to chat to, then doing it very well. I didn't find public speaking difficult, as it felt to me like an abstract activity; it was the more intimate conversations that led to getting jobs and then getting cases which worried me.

So, instead of going on to do professional training, I did another degree, this time in philosophy, and then wrote a doctorate in legal theory. The doctorate was a form of professional training too – I expected that I would continue teaching and researching in the same field and that this would be my career. However, by this stage, I had also moved away from home. I went four hundred miles away – one hour by plane – to do my PhD. And, on arriving there, I decided to do things differently.

During law school, I had the experiences with conversation that I have described. And for the first time, being clever began to mean that the world was more decipherable – knowing about law and philosophy, and being good with both, meant that I could read newspapers more closely than before; I could work out the context to ideas; when someone made a point, I knew what the opposite of it was or where it might lead to. I was emboldened by this and so when I moved, I decided that I would do things differently.

My father drove me down the first time with my things. I spoke to the shop assistant at one of the service stations on the motorway. As soon as we arrived, I bumped into another new graduate student and I was able to talk to him about his work, about his journey; I humorously compared our fathers checking the oil in their car engines, proud that they had done the right thing by their sons. Suddenly, it wasn't just a resolution, it was how I could be in my new place.

Three years later, as I rewrote my entire thesis for the final time – my response to criticism is often out of proportion, I destroy an artefact that represents what was criticized and start again (this is done almost ceremonially, past examples have included: printing out the pages and folding each page into a plane which was then thrown out of a window into the back garden; trying to feed a floppy disk to a colony of ants; sawing through a tennis racket) – my ambition of becoming an academic was succeeded by another acceptance of my added abilities. I had spent my entire adult life in universities and I had gotten good at being in them, but, at the same time, I had also gotten good at other things. I knew a lot about politics at this stage. I had read a lot. With a training in both law and philosophy, I was horrible to argue against. And so I started looking for a job in a sphere where I could apply these skills. I found the UK Civil Service; I'm still there.

Craig snapped his notebook shut and stood. 'People should have stayed for longer,' I suddenly realized. 'People should have stayed for longer and chatted to one another,' I explained. The end of the speech had felt a little too much like the end of a play. There was applause, some stamping of feet against the ground (so it was probably a very good play), but there was no continuing tumult. Senator Kerry left, and the crowd started to leave too. I wanted strangers to turn to one another and say, 'I liked this bit, but not that bit'; 'Can we call it a doctrine yet?'; to mention names of international relations scholars and assess who Kerry and his team were reading and who they should be reading.

Craig shrugged his shoulders. His pen was still in his hand and he was clicking it open and shut repeatedly. He was excited about the lines that he had written.

'Let's go,' I conceded.

★

We left the car on the street and walked up the driveway towards the house. We were on our way to a Republican fundraiser on Long Island, holding invitation cards with our names embossed in gold letters. The driveway was twisty, with tall trees on either side; the house was massive, lit up, and I thought that our evening would more closely resemble *The Great Gatsby* if we left the car on the street and walked. Craig had not read the book though and he had not seen the film, so my insistence, and my description of Robert Redford in a pink silk suit, raised an eyebrow but produced no profound effect.

I was nervous. Impulsively, I had blagged tickets for the fundraiser from a friend who was a Republican. It had seemed, in the abstract, that it might be a fun occasion: we could start arguments with them, savour their foibles; they would probably have excellent canapés. Now that we were actually going, I was acquiring a series of concerns. I wasn't convinced that my shoes were smart enough for the occasion. They were suede. Could you wear suede to a Republican do on Long Island? I had also begun to suspect that we were obvious, or so it felt, Democrat-types and that this might be noticed almost straightaway. I was most nervous, however, because Craig was walking much slower than me. Suddenly he stopped. He stood, with the palm of his left hand against a tree. He was looking down at the ground.

*

We had spent the afternoon in his apartment. It resembled the apartment of a cinema serial killer. When he was writing, whenever he found something useful in a newspaper, he'd rip out the page and stick it to a spare piece of wall. But he didn't always take the pages down when he was finished so the walls were littered with irregular strips of newspaper. There was a stack of old notebooks on the kitchen table and it wasn't clear why they needed to be there, especially as the table already carried a spare computer and most of an old edition of the *Encyclopaedia Britannica*. It was very clean, however. Everything was very clean.

Living alone hadn't been his idea but, four years ago, his parents had agreed to try restoring their marriage through a trial separation. There was a two-day moratorium after they told him about it, but then they both started lobbying him, both contending that he should come stay with one rather than the other. Craig found this really difficult. It had never occurred to him that he would need to live away from his parents and though he was quite independent in some ways – he never asked his parents to review letters that he wrote, he told them about his job prospects but rarely sought their advice on which opportunities to pursue – living alone sounded perilous and complicated. He had a vague sense that his parents did lots of things around the house that needed to be done but which he didn't understand. Sometimes he helped with grocery shopping, but he did it from a list and, when he came home, he left the bags at the breakfast bar in the kitchen – he lacked a sense of the connection between the shopping that he had done and the meal that was cooked that night.

It was his grandmother who decided that, under the circumstances, he would need to live on his own. Craig was using her as a confidant during this period and then, on one occasion, when he was talking to her on the phone in the living-room, his parents arrived home while still having an argument. It was a loud one and his grandmother began to overhear some of it. She asked him to put the speaker on so that she could hear it better. It raged for about an hour. When it finished, she asked Craig to put the speaker off. When he came back on the line, she told him that she was coming and that she'd be there by the evening.

When she arrived, she did so with papers from three different letting agents. She sat his parents down and explained that what they were doing to him was wrong and that they needed to let him live on his own while they sorted things out; they mustn't involve him in their tussle. She then led Craig upstairs to his room and they chose a flat for him to live in. She stayed with him for the first four weeks – she taught him how to cook five basic dishes; she showed him how to wipe down the shower cubicle every morning after he'd used it to avoid the build-up of watermarks on the glass; he acquired enough new knowledge to feel that this new prospect of living on his own was manageable, at least while his parents sought to resolve their differences.

His grandmother came to visit him every weekend for the first six months. But even she was impressed at how well he managed. He didn't make some of the obvious mistakes that boys living on their own for the first time make. He liked cleanliness and so he always took out the garbage; he didn't have many close friends and so the flat never became littered with cartons of takeaway food or cans of beer. What he found hardest was something that he would never have expected to find difficult: spending so much time on his own. He came to realize that, without having other people around, evenings could be really long. He'd come home from work, change his clothes neatly, cook a meal, eat it in front of the television, wash the dishes – he'd do all this and discover that just forty-five minutes had passed. Evenings were much longer than forty-five minutes. He didn't always want to read and even watching the news channels didn't work, as all the stories began to reappear after about half an hour.

It was during this time, to finish off long evenings, that Craig began calling people for social reasons for the first time in his life. He'd call friends from work or cousins or even one of his parents. He'd call for no particular reason but just to talk. And then, he went from talking to them on the telephone to meeting up with them. He began meeting his mother for dinner twice a week. He spent Sundays with his father. He joined a Wednesday evening Latin class – to refresh what he had been taught by the Jesuits many years ago – with an aide to a senator that he wrote for regularly. His grandmother noted all of this happening and, when his parents decided to make a second go of it and asked him to move back in with them, she took him out for lunch and asked him whether he felt like he had a choice. He didn't immediately understand what she meant and so she asked him again, 'Do you realize that you can choose to keep living in your own apartment?' Later that week, he went home to his parents and explained that he really loved them – his grandmother had advised him to start with that – he was delighted that they were back together, he'd be over several times a week, but he was earning more than enough money for the rent and he was going to stay where he was.

After Craig had shown me all his bookshelves and made sure that I knew how many books there were in total, we settled down on the sofa to watch some tapes of Craig delivering speeches. These were critical, I felt. Just as André used puppets to express himself, Craig used the speeches of other people. But while André's puppets all spoke as flatly as he did, I expected to hear, on these tapes, Craig's emphases and enthusiasms. He wrote powerful speeches; I had read about a dozen of them. He must know that he did, he must convey that in his performances, he must use these tapes to chart the rip tides of his sentences.

'What do you want to watch?' Craig asked. He listed a series of politicians and dates. I put my feet up on the sofa and threw the responsibility back to him. He rubbed his brow a bit and chose a tape from the end of the stack.

On screen, the lectern was empty. Craig came into the shot, carrying a portfolio. He set it down and made an empty wave, delivered a smile. He said, 'Thank you', amplified it with, 'Thank you very much', and then started to read from his pages. It was a speech about energy policy. He opened by describing a scenario whereby Saudi Arabia cut off oil supplies to the United States. He described the period during which domestic oil reserves were being used up not as 'the calm before the storm' – an expression which would have come to him too quickly, I think, would have made him feel that he was being generic and not engaging with what precisely was at stake – but as 'the moments between when you've lost your footing but you've yet to hit the ground'. He then spoke about machinery coming to a halt, lost tempers outside gas stations, frantic motions on the stock market floor. The imagery was thorough and iconic. The language was bare, but gripping. And it was only when he began to explain why drilling in Alaska really wasn't going to help with this enough, three minutes into his speech – there was a timer in the top right-hand corner of the screen – that I noticed that he was speaking as he usually spoke, except possibly a little louder.

*

Craig had moved to standing with his back against the tree. He was pretending that he was pausing longer only to look at the moon. I shouldn't have been surprised by the onset of his anxiety, but I was. I'd seen him impress the senatorial aide on the steps outside Columbia Library. He was very fluent on the telephone. And so, even though he'd told me about not being able to deliver the graduation speech in high school, though he'd told me about how quietly college went, though he'd told me about the interview in which he started drumming, I was surprised that we were still by the tree and I realized that I had opted for the optimistic version. Craig was obviously a high-functioning autistic person. Autism is a spectrum and Craig was on a different point of it to both André and Randall. But I needed not to forget that he was nevertheless on it.

I was anxious too. I was anxious that a discerning someone at the party would out us as Democrats. I was anxious to be wearing suede shoes. And now I was anxious about being

Craig's chaperone. It wasn't a role that I had ever played. I had watched Amanda do it with André. I had watched Mike do it with Randall. It was something that other people did with me. I had self-appointed big sisters all through high school and college. I relied on other people to introduce me and bring me into conversations. I relied on other people turning up at my door and making sure that I went to the party after all. I had no experience of being the carer.

I was afraid that anything that I might say to Craig would sound patronizing. I'd thought that of things other people had said to me. But they were welcome nonetheless. So I said, 'Let's set some targets. For example, whenever we get into a row about energy policy up there, as soon as the discussant mentions drilling in Alaska, that's a point.'

Craig smiled. 'I like that.'

'Will you keep score?' I asked, trying to draw him further into the game.

'As soon as they say tax cuts stimulate the economy, that's a point,' he suggested.

'Half a point. Otherwise, it's too easy.'

'OK, OK. As soon as they make the Bush–Reagan comparison, that's a point.'

'That's definitely a point. Agreed. And any accusations of Democrat voter fraud, that's a point.'

'The country's ripe with it; you know that, don't you?' he asked me, smiling now.

'Individuals giving money through the Internet. Can you imagine? How are corporations supposed to keep a grip on their candidates?'

Craig laughed. 'That's a point.'

I had no idea what to do next. This was a fun conversation

but it wasn't necessarily going to get us up the remainder of the driveway to the house with the blazing bulbs so we could use our plush invitation cards. Craig hadn't moved. His animation was limited in its effect to the ideas he was generating. Finally, I started walking.

'A point for any word or phrase that actually means black people,' I continued.

'You mean people from depressed urban areas who've become dependent on welfare,' Craig replied, pulling up beside me.

'That's a point.' I almost sighed, a little with gratitude, a little with dread, for I felt like I'd tricked him, like I'd crushed up a pill and sprinkled it on his food. Why were we going to this anyway? Wasn't it just a lot of trouble? Craig tried to go to as many such events as he could. Being a successful speech-writer, especially a freelance one, as he was for the moment, depended on brokering and keeping up contacts. He did this fairly well and he had people who looked after him at events such as this one. But this one wasn't going to expand his Rolodex – wrong political party – and I couldn't introduce him to people, which was what he was used to. Nevertheless, we were on our way now and I tried to remember some of the reasons why we had thought that it would be fun.

I failed, and instead I thought about what Craig had told me the night before, that he had never been in a long-term relationship. We had stayed up until late drawing graphs based on polling figures across one of the walls in his apartment. The girl that he had dated for the longest – nine months – had been a pollster. She began going through a difficult time at work. Her boss was going through a divorce and was tetchy at work, there less and less; he stopped giving positive feedback, snapped at her for minor mistakes. Though she disliked herself for it, this began to affect her performance and a sort of cycle developed. She explained this to Craig regularly. He made suggestions, he met her after work in a café that she liked, he booked a holiday. There were good days, but no broader improvement and she felt under constant strain. She felt too that she was hogging all of the time in which they talked about their days at work; she felt that Craig stopped sharing things with her as a consequence of her unhappiness and this made her angry with him, emphasized the distance between them. She explained this to him and, after each time that she did, he tried to correct the balance for a little while, but then dropped into the role of listener again. Craig believed that this was the right thing to do and, anyway, it was what he felt more comfortable doing. But she knew that and she had always feared, since the beginning of their relationship, that he would resile from her – she figured that in a relationship with an autistic person, this was bound to be one of the points of stress. When it happened, even though it was for what Craig thought were good reasons, she left.

Obviously, any relationship might crack open under these circumstances, but it was hard for Craig to see it that way; it was hard for autistic people like him and me to convince ourselves that something like this didn't happen because of the autism. Craig had talked me through this and I had agreed. I wasn't able to say very much more in response – I was tired, something similar had happened to me once; it made me sad to hear another version of it from a person who was becoming a friend. And now, of course,

I was bringing him to a party that was going to be difficult, for both of us.

We walked through the entrance and came into a vast hallway. I glanced at Craig's expression out of the edge of my eye but he seemed OK – he was taking it in. I began to imagine that all the doors led to closets, not rooms, that all the acreage had been spent on the hallway. The guests were dressed in suits or blazers or sports jackets and no one was wearing suede shoes. Most people looked like they had been glazed with a paintbrush dipped in egg yolk. We were late and the party had already begun to settle into clumps. There was a group of young men, one of whom kept unsettling, without fully upsetting, a small table by the stairs but wouldn't move from his spot in their circle – they all carried a bearing like they ought to have a pet panther with them. Craig and I did an orbit around the ground floor of the house. We found that it was possible to walk under the stairs, that there was an enormous fireplace there with armchairs before it and that the canapés were excellent, as we had hoped. The milieu satisfied my *Great Gatsby* yearnings, though there were few women and no prospect of a dance.

As we walked around, we looked for ways to enter conversations. But no one seemed to be talking about the campaign, or about politics at all. There was a conversation about soybeans, around which we paused, anticipating a discussion of agricultural policy, but it quickly turned into an anecdote about a relative's farm; there was a conversation about Mizen Head, the southernmost point in Ireland; there was a conversation about ice-skating in Central Park.

The next time I looked across at Craig, he looked glum. I wasn't surprised. His career in politics rested on being able to write well, to write well on the issues. He got work because of this ability, not because he was a member of a high-profile golfing pack or was invited to supper by prominent families. He ought to feel a kinship to other people involved in politics, involved enough to come to a fund-raiser, but he would feel no tie to the people we were meeting at this party. We had known that this was going to be the difficult part – making conversation with Republicans – but we had thought it would be difficult because we'd have to be careful about how clearly we expressed our dissent; we never imagined that there'd be no Republican politics at a Republican fund-raiser. What were we going to do now? I at least had brought a crocodile clip with me to help me out.

I opened the clip and I closed it. I opened it and held it open. I put a finger between its jaws and let go its sides. I released my finger and placed the clip briefly in the palm of my hand. The crocodile clip provided what I described before as local coherence. I could focus on what I was doing with the clip and other matters could become just a back-drop. I didn't have to worry about what I was achieving at the party. I could take a break and worry about the clip instead, which was a simpler thing to worry about, a simpler thing to understand and to manipulate. I felt that I had deceived Craig by snagging him in a conversation when he paused by the tree; the crocodile clip was for self-deception.

I turned the clip over, rolling it between my fingers in my trouser pocket. I was trying to plot my next move, imagine another stratagem. Then Craig spotted someone he had written with before and strode over. I was alarmed. Wouldn't this person know that Craig was a Democrat? But they were pleased to see one another and gladly shook hands.

'I'm here with a friend; plus my parents live near here,' announced Craig's former colleague.

'My uncle lives on Long Island,' Craig said, excusing himself too. We had found another secret Democrat. After I had introduced myself, Craig told him about the points system, and we agreed that he could play too.

Craig and he stayed in each other's apartments. As Craig lived in New York, there were often times when he made an overnight stay in Washington DC, and some of his friends likewise were regularly in New York for their work. Initially, Craig had stayed in hotels every time he went to Washington. He liked hotels and was used to them from traveling with his parents. There was a particular hotel in the capital that he returned to every time he needed it and, when in other cities, he stayed in hotels belonging to the same franchise. Hotel rooms were regular, unlike other people's houses. In other people's houses, there was always some idiosyncrasy to do with the shower ('pull the curtain all the way along to the left or the water'll drip on the floor'; 'turn the knob on the left-hand side a couple of times – if you turn it three times, you've gone too far – and then turn the lever in the middle counter-clockwise'), or you didn't know if you would be offered a towel or not and it was hard to clarify that beforehand on the phone. However, Craig found that though his friends might stay with him a couple of times, when he kept refusing their offers of a room, they eventually stopped staying with him too.

This provided Craig with a dilemma. He had begun to like the sense of capability that he got from having a guest in the house, and so he compromised: he started staying 'yes' to the offers and when the Washington hotel rang to check if he was dissatisfied with their service, he wrote them a letter explaining all the things that they did tremendously well and the reason why he had stopped staying with them. But staying in other people's houses, interacting with a different set of personal effects and a wide range of objects all with stories behind them that he didn't know remained difficult – why was there a chipped mug sitting on the mantelpiece? where did the wooden model come from that was put together squiffy? – so he devised a strategy to help him to manage. Every time he stayed with a friend, he reordered one thing. For example, if there was a pile of books on the coffee table, he might pick it up and alphabetize it; if the flowers in the vases were a little crumbly, he might go out and buy a whole set of fresh ones. After he had done this one thing, introduced this coherence of his own, he came back to it every time he began to feel a little anxious. The last time that he had stayed with the friend we just met, he had dismantled a pedestal fan that wasn't circulating properly and fixed it.

An hour and a half later, we were out on the patio talking to the young men who had been standing by the stairs when we came in. I had scored a point, but the others had scored zero. It was bizarre. There wasn't an argument to be had in the entire place. Everyone was being pleasant, without strain. Whenever we got a chance to test people's views, they were either sure that Bush was going to win or that the issues weren't what was going to settle it. Our experiment in political agitprop had been a flop. Instead, Craig was now telling jokes, alternating with one of the sharp-faced Republican men, who seemed to have just as many to work through. I hadn't seen Craig like this. I didn't know that he told jokes. His tone still didn't change, he didn't yammer out the jokes, he didn't put on voices, but he had good ones and they worked. He finished the joke and he laughed after each one. No doubt the men we had met were thinking other things too, about this person who told jokes while looking at his feet and then laughed really hard to support these contributions, but mostly they were just laughing, and contributing with side-remarks, and one of them was matching Craig gag for gag.

After the party, we walked back to his uncle's house, exulted. We'd had a good time. I had only taken the crocodile clip out of my pocket on one occasion. We left with other people's business cards, maybe three or four each. Our sense of achievement was, to be level-headed about it, an inflated one. After all, it was just a drinks reception. Everyone had handed out cards to one another. We hadn't talked to that many people and we weren't the last to leave. Still, we felt pretty triumphant. We had gone to a party for the politics and had managed even though, in the event, there'd been no politics. We turned into a small lane – I remembered it from earlier in the day – and we were faced with the moon again. Craig put his hands on his head and shouted, 'Send in the Idiots.' We repeated it two or three times and then made the rest of our way home.

*

It happened in Ohio, in the end, though forecasters had thought it might be Florida, Pennsylvania, Wisconsin, or even Hawaii. We watched it on different sides of the Atlantic Ocean. I was back in London. Craig was outside Senator Kerry's house near Boston. We spoke by cell phone several times during the night.

The results of the US presidential election on November 3rd 2004 were devastating for us. It's too easy to say this the wrong way. It wasn't that we thought that stupidity had won out over intelligence, or fear over hope, or xenophobia over liberal ambition. Maybe we thought that too but, even if we did, those are political disappointments, reversible ones – our side didn't win the argument and that should toughen our resolve to make the argument better next time. What we felt, more acutely, was that there was no room for us, for Craig and me, in the jobs that we worked; if November 3rd 2004 represented the dominant version of political affairs, we might need to find something else to do.

Take the example of partial birth abortion. It aptly illustrates the different versions of political affairs that the two candidates, President Bush and Senator Kerry, represented.

President Bush spoke against partial birth abortion. Whenever he gave his view, he was placid and straightforward, as if he was telling you his shoe size. In two of the televised debates, he pulled up Senator Kerry for voting against a bill in the US Senate to ban partial birth abortion. Kerry explained that he was opposed to partial birth abortion. However, the legislation had contained no exemption for cases where there was rape or incest involved; as a consequence, he had voted against the Bill. Bush turned on this explanation. He shook his head: you're either for it or against it. Kerry shook his head too: it's not as simple as that.

Of course, it can be as simple as that. There's a perfectly good argument that states that a fetus is a human life and that, regardless of the circumstances, you're not morally permitted to take active steps to end a human life. President Bush may have been alluding to this argument. However, he didn't try to put across this argument. He didn't try to help people see the force of it. Instead, his tactic was a different one.

Senator Kerry had just tried to reflect the complexity of the issue, to vex those people who may otherwise oppose a ban on partial birth abortion, to urge them to stop and think about the detail. President Bush was trying to halt that process. He was telling those viewers: no, it's as easy as you thought it was, you're allowed to be as firm as you want to be on this one; there are only two answers, and my opponent has the wrong one. At the same time, President Bush succeeded in sending a signal to those who supported his position, who didn't even waver on hearing Senator Kerry's argument: watch out, he's tricksy, but I'm straight with you, and I know, like you, what's right and what's wrong.

The version of political affairs by which President Bush was re-elected on November 3rd 2004 gives primacy to affinity, not argument. Craig and I have based our careers on the latter. That night, as the full force of the Republican victory became apparent, that basis felt deeply eroded.

President Bush had the opportunity, when it came to partial birth abortion, when it came to any number of issues, to state the arguments that he and his supporters espoused or ought to espouse in order to justify the positions that they take. However, he didn't state the arguments. He didn't explain why Senator Kerry's reasons for voting against the abortion ban were bad reasons. He didn't explain how Saddam Hussein's government was connected to the terrorist attacks on September 11th 2001. He didn't need to. He and his campaign knew that enough people believed that abortion was wrong. He and his campaign knew that enough people believed that there were links between Iraq and Al-Qaeda. And, among those people who didn't believe that, there were enough other people who didn't want to take the risk of insisting that there was no link or that Iraq was no threat to the security of the USA. There was enough belief and enough fear, and argument didn't get a look-in.

The problem for Craig and me is that we can only do argument. We don't have the wherewithal for creating or sustaining affinity. When we write a speech, it's argument that we look for. We need there to be a chain of reasoning between the paragraphs. We need there to be a structure. When Craig met the aide in front of Columbia Library, for example, he asked for quotations from the judge who was being honored in the speech. He wanted to use a quotation that made three points, or invoked three values, to split the speech into three parts. This is how our minds work.

In one sense, it's another manifestation of the desire for local coherence; it's also the inability to write another way. Craig writes powerful speeches, but they are powerful because he understands rhetorical tools and their power is enhanced if the arguments are sound. His speeches are not powerful by virtue of being emotionally affecting. Otherwise, when he records himself, he would need to assess whether his performance made an emotional impact. He doesn't do that. He doesn't seek in his own performance of a speech to create an emotional impact. Instead, he is checking whether the rhetorical tools work, whether certain lines scan correctly, whether there are leaps between paragraphs that don't succeed when the speech is read aloud.

I don't dismiss the other version of political affairs.

Because it is different from mine, and less accessible to me, because it is successful, I'm actually quite drawn to it – at least, I'd like to know it better.

Certainly, I don't think that it's about stupidity. The day after the election, I received, as did millions of people, emails with links to tables showing that lower average IQ scores, across the states of America, corresponded to higher shares of the vote for President Bush. There are several collections of Bush-isms, such as, 'The French have no word for entrepreneur' or, 'Do not misunderestimate me'. It's perfectly possible to point to Americans who couldn't find Iraq or the UK on a map, and sigh in despair. But I don't think that the politics of affinity have succeeded because they exploit stupidity.

However, I do think that they exploit ignorance – except it may be a respectable form of ignorance. For people like Craig and me, politics is a professional activity. We get paid to do it. Most of our friends do it. We studied politics, and subjects related to it, at university. I don't think that we should be appalled if other people, people for whom it isn't a vocation, know less about politics or care less about politics.

Plainly, they do. Turnout at the 2004 US presidential election was fifty-four per cent. While commentators conventionally referred to it as the most important election in years, barely every second person voted. Turnout levels in the UK are similar. You might think that people are more interested in local affairs, which intersect with their own lives more often, but turnout levels in local elections are even lower, sometimes by half as much again. Ordinary people have the opportunity to act as school governors, sit on hospital boards, or become community magistrates –

government is really keen for them to do so and continues to create new decision-making fora at the local level – but these posts often go unfilled.

The Freedom of Information Act in the UK provides another important illustration of disinterest. The act allows, as of January 1st 2005, any person to request any information from any public authority. The right of access conferred by the act extends to all information held by public authorities, not just information created since the implementation of the act. Most requests are free. The definition of public authorities includes central and local government, schools, healthcare trusts, police forces, and many archives – over 100,000 bodies in total. So, if you want to know what plans your local authority has for the care home in which your mother resides, ask. If you want to find out more about the schools in your local area, ask. If you want the costs analysis on the options available to the Secretary of State for Transport for road-building that affects your commute to work, ask. Government has never been so transparent before.

Set all of this against survey work done towards the end of 2004, though, which showed that only around twenty per cent of people were aware of these new access rights and that only six per cent of people expected to make a request for information. The entire public sector issues a universal invitation to ask any question for free, and not even one person in ten can imagine writing an email to exercise this new right.

Many other countries, including Australia, Canada, Ireland and the US, had freedom of information laws before the UK. Their experiences are revealingly similar. Only five per cent of Australian citizens have ever made a request. Sixty-two per cent of public authorities in Canada have never received a request. Freedom of information can only deliver the changes in political culture that government promises if citizens respond by making requests. This is an opportunity for citizen-driven change, but citizens aren't interested.

Though it has become commonplace to agonize about low levels of trust in government and politicians, arguably the figures on turnout and on freedom of information suggest the opposite. People are happy for political affairs to be run by a professional class. Turnout is low because people think things are going well enough or, at least, they're not willing to make changes in their own lives, to devote less time to their private interests, in order to take a more active role in political affairs. They don't want to engage in politics in a thorough way and so politicians don't have to try to engage them in that way. The Bush campaign had it right. People want to elect someone who broadly shares their outlook, who seems to be responsive to their fears, who is straightforward and therefore worthy of their trust. They don't want to get into arguments. Some matter might be more complicated, but that's not their business – they don't want to hear that it's more complicated, they want the person that they elect to be sure.

Is this an unreasonable attitude? I don't think it is. People like Craig and I shouldn't expect everyone to share our interests. After all, architects don't expect people to notice different types of stone or explain the structural splendor of an atrium. Dentists don't expect people to be able to name all the different types of tooth or understand the nervous system that runs beneath them.

However, disinterest or disengagement, when it comes to

politics, is more worrying. Politics is more significant than dentistry; politics might be about how the entire healthcare system turns out. And the problem is that it is possible for a candidate to come across as trustworthy, reliable, right-on, but only on listening to the detail will you realize how bogus the rhetoric is, or how flawed the arguments. Within the politics of affinity, rather than that of argument, it may be more difficult to discern quality, or to cut through the crap. The Republican lie about a connection between Saddam Hussein and 9/11, and their systematic misrepresentation of Senator Kerry's voting record, are just two examples of political rhetoric that wasn't tested as hard as it should have been.

It's also a problem if the disengagement is localized to minority or disadvantaged communities. If there is an élite class that is engaged, that has access to politicians, and thereby whose views carry weight when there are other populations whose views don't, then democracy is in danger. Representation is less than exact. There must also come a point at which turnout and other forms of participation are so low that government's mandate becomes too thin; it becomes incredible for government to claim that it is carrying out the will of the people.

Unfortunately, and it felt this way especially on November 3rd 2004 – as the result in Ohio became clear, and Craig and I stood in corners of crowded rooms, unable to say anything to one another via our cell phones, and yet unwilling to leave each other's company – these problems are not theoretical.

November 3rd 2004 therefore presented an urgent challenge for progressive politics in the US. Our insides hummed like tuning forks with the realization of it. President Bush, and the politics of affinity, had won. And won well. The Democrats had suffered in congressional elections too. Even their hegemony in California – the state with the most electoral college votes, the state without which Democrats can't launch a realistic bid for the White House – began to look a little shaky. Did this mean that the politics of argument had to be ditched? Did progressives need to bore in on affinity too? Craig and I felt that our side had won the argument so convincingly, and yet lost the contest so dismally, that the version of political affairs in which we could participate was about to expire. For its own future well-being, our side needed to let it, and us, go. For Craig, especially, the next few months were incredibly difficult. He kept failing in interviews, like the one in which he started drumming on his chair. His letters and emails went un-answered. No doubt there were other reasons for this too. The Democrats he was writing to were disillusioned. The next election cycle was a long way off. There were other candidates, also cast off from election campaigns, with broader experiences or better connections. However, it all felt continuous to him; it all felt like it was related to a loss of faith in argument and so a loss of faith in people like him.

Of course, none of this is so dichotomous. Democrats aspire to the affinity of voters too. They traditionally take a higher proportion of the vote among many minority com-munities and that has a lot to do with affinity. Progressive politicians, both in the US and elsewhere, appeal to the softer side in people. I've written speeches of that ilk. I feel less comfortable doing it, but I've tried. It feels inauthentic to me, but maybe it also feels inauthentic to the speaker, needing to describe a set of minor but well-thought-through reforms as a 'revolution' or a 'new era', to invoke 'destiny' rather than 'diligence'. And sometimes people on the right make an argument. Sometimes it's not a bad one. But everything felt starker than this on the night of November 3rd 2004. And neither Craig nor I will lose that feeling. Craig still doesn't have a job; I've kept mine, but I'm a civil servant – it's hard to lose it.

It's possible, in some lasting sense, that the Idiots have been sent out of politics.

*

'Do you whistle?'

'No,' admitted Craig.

'I feel like we should be whistling,' I said, tearing out a blade of grass.

'Do you whistle?' Craig asked.

'I have about the worst whistle in the entire history of whistling.'

Craig nodded. There was a conversation lurking about the boy-style things we didn't know how to do – whistle, rig a sail, fight – and the consequences of these incapacitites. We weren't keen to have it, but the last silence had been a long one, and it did feel like a time for whistling.

We were sitting on the grass by Stonehenge. It was two days before the winter solstice and there were a lot of people around. There was a woman with a guitar but she wasn't playing. She was sitting with it in her lap, her hands hovering over the right places, as if she was composing or waiting for the light to strike the stones in a particular way.

Craig was jobless still. On the verge of the holidays, he had run out of interviews to go to. New jobs were taking some time to emerge after the election; there was a real chance that it would take the Democrats at least a year to begin rebuilding properly. Craig had already written the covering letters he intended to send in January and had stopped writing phrases or ideas in his notebook for lines to take; it was possible, he felt, that he ought to use the time and his savings in order to travel. Even so, getting him to come to the UK had taken a lot of persuasion. And, over here, mostly he was sleeping and skimming through the books in my study. Though he lived alone, this was the first overseas trip that he had made on his own. He wasn't doing too well at being out of his routines. On arriving in London, he had walked out of the departure lounge without his luggage and it had been a kerfuffle to get him back in to find it. He didn't want to meet any of my friends. He'd ask me to brief him, so I'd sit with him and set out their interests, likely topics of conversation; a couple of times we got as far as the tube station but then he'd decline, with apologies, though without meeting my eyes. It seemed to me that he didn't understand really why they wanted to meet him, or why I wanted him to meet them. He was my friend, after all, not theirs. He was only a visitor and so there was no scope for developing any conversations that they may continue later. As a consequence, we mostly stayed indoors. Stonehenge was the one place that he had asked to visit; he remembered it from a children's television show.

We were surprised by Stonehenge. There wasn't very much to read and we didn't want to get locked into an audio guide. We walked around the monument once and sat down on the grass. I tried to imagine how the stones would have been brought there, but I couldn't. Craig was idly observing the woman with the guitar. I was afraid that I hadn't planned this trip well enough. I hadn't planned it at all. We had only hired the car that morning. I had suggested that we drive on to Bath, but it would be early evening at least by the time we got there, and I hadn't booked a hotel room.

I tugged on one of Craig's laces. His parents had told him that he and I used to do this to one another a lot when we were in school together and, since he had been over, we had started again. Strangely, I didn't remember doing it back then. I didn't remember much about Craig. I also still didn't know him very well. Part of the problem was that, even though Craig was staying with me and we were spending a lot of time together, it was very hard to get him to talk about topics other than politics, including himself. Perhaps he saw our friendship that way, that we had become friends on meeting each other again because we shared an interest in politics and so that was what we should talk about; perhaps he thought that I expected him to talk about politics and that I didn't want him to talk about anything else.

This was far from the truth. Instead I was worried about Craig. I was worried that he was still in love with the girl who had broken up with him during her period of work-related depression. At one point, my home phone rang but the caller hung up just as I got to it. Craig asked me whether it was her. I checked for the caller's number but it had been withheld. I told him that it was probably my mother – who sometimes dialled my number by mistake, as it was similar to the number of one of her friends – and that her phone number always came up as 'withheld'. He was disappointed by my suggestion and explained that he had emailed his former girlfriend my number as it'd be cheaper for her than calling his cell phone and, though there was no reason for her to call, she may do so. On the back of this, I tried to ask him more about her, but then he stopped talking and decided to go for a walk.

I was also worried about what he would do for work. It didn't sound like he was even coming close in any of his interviews and there really would be minimal speech-writing work for the foreseeable future. I kept printing out the details of policy seminars happening in London; I suppose I had this fantasy that he would go to one of these, ask a stunning question, talk to the right person afterwards, and that this would lead to something. But he didn't go to any of them. Sometimes he promised to go and, when I came home from work, he'd be lying on the sofa again and it'd be obvious that he hadn't left the house all day.

It might almost have been simpler if we'd never known each other. Though we had spent a lot of time together in the US, gone to campaign events and stayed up late debating issues, done things that were sufficient to open a friendship, there was also a set of precedents from our earlier friendship as children. We felt that we needed to adhere to these in some way but we didn't remember our earlier friendship and our parents recollected it in the partial anecdotes of parents. These were like holiday snaps or the official pictures taken at the start of a formal social event – only accidentally did they give us any sort of basis. We knew that we pulled one another's laces, but we didn't know why we started doing that, whether we ever used it to annoy one another, whether it caused fights, whether the practice spread, why we stopped. Like with the stones where we were sitting before, there was a bundle of process stories, but we didn't know what they were.

So we continued to stare at the stones and take in the people around us. There were a number of parents with their children. There were a number of groups. For those of us sitting on the grass, set away from the monument, the people walking around the stones – many wearing the black head-phones of the audio guide – were becoming part of the spectacle. It was like an exhibit in a zoo, with a sham landscape thrown together to fool the captives; there was even a wire fence running alongside the road.

I turned to Craig and pulled the laces on his other shoe. He'd already untied both of mine.

'Are you getting this?' I asked.

He shook his head, reluctantly, or slowly.

'Perhaps we should get a book from the shop,' I suggested. 'Or do you have a book already?'

He recrossed his legs. He tore off a handful of grass and began to sort through it on his palm. 'I thought this might be the one place we could try to sit without a book,' he shrugged.

'Oh,' I realized, after a pause. Suddenly I felt bad, like when you haven't been thinking about the time and then you're late for an appointment with a friend; you feel like you've let them down and you don't have an excuse. Craig was trying and I had just failed to acknowledge the effort that he was making. 'I'm sorry, Craig.'

He shook his head in protest. 'I should learn to say what I'm thinking,' he murmured.

'You shouldn't need to say it to me,' I replied firmly. 'I don't want to be another person whose expectations you need to manage.' It had suddenly struck me that Craig didn't want to go on trips and this meant that I should stop mentioning it. He didn't want to meet my friends and I should stop trying to make him. I was Craig's autistic ally. Perhaps we had developed to different points in the autism spectrum, but I didn't want to be so far from him that he needed to explain to me why he was worried about going to a party, or ask me whether it was OK to just order in a pizza. I still had the same anxieties. Hadn't I said that clearly enough? Hadn't we tried hard enough to establish that we were still similar? I really didn't want to jeopardize the prospect of us properly becoming friends. I felt cross. I stood up. It might help to walk.

'Wait,' exclaimed Craig. He remembered that my laces were untied. He began to do them up. I didn't move. I watched him tie my laces.

When he had finished, I asked, 'Shall we go?'

Taking another handful of grass tops, he replied, 'Let's stay until the sun sets. I think that's what the other people are waiting for.'

I nodded. Perhaps the woman with the guitar would play a song then. Perhaps some of the stones would move. 'In that case, I'm going to get some ice cream,' I declared. Craig nodded and gave me an exaggerated wave goodbye.

'Hey,' I said.

'Hey,' he replied.

4

'WHY DID YOU GET BETTER?'

I heard these words and I felt as if I must have fallen asleep. Immediately I started replaying the question in my head, trying to work out the tone in which it was asked. He let me. We sat silently for a while and then he got up to make himself a drink. His wife had disappeared into the house somewhere. It was easier when she was in the room. She talked more than he did and provided a commentary on any remarks that he made.

He'd been drinking for most of the evening. Not fast, or recklessly, but it was clear that this was what he was doing – the time was structured into episodes, each of which began with making a drink. He did this carefully, with his back to the room. He removed the caps of the bottles. He measured out the different ingredients. He stirred them together. Each stage was distinct and it had all his attention. Then he sat down and put the drink by his chair. After a pause, he took his first sip from it and cleared his throat. Clearing his throat was the stage direction, the page break; it was him calling the meeting to order – it meant he was listening again.

As he came back towards his chair from the drinks cabinet, he moved as if the room was dark, or as if he was in a funhouse at a fair, and it was likely that furniture would suddenly start crashing around, or a skeleton would drop down from the ceiling. I hadn't yet thought of what to say in answer to his question and he would shortly be clearing his throat. I uncrossed my legs and rubbed my right thigh. I was slightly afraid of him. He was a professor of history and – because he was drunk, and because earlier in the evening his wife had corrected him when he forgot things – I suspected that he wanted me to underestimate him, to think him doddering, and give a patronizing or simplistic answer. Then he'd wipe the floor with me and they wouldn't ask me back to the house. Earlier, we'd been listening to the news, and he had leapt off from a comment that a reporter made about local politics in Indonesia and explained what the tension in that region really was. He spoke as if he was reading out a passage of his own prose that he had read many times before – it almost scanned, he paused well – but he wasn't, he was just talking.

He sat down. He cleared his throat and changed the question slightly.

'Did everyone get better?'

An odd wave of relief passed through me. 'No, sir,' I replied.

Several of the people I contacted for this book didn't want to be in it. Often, it was their parents who turned me down. Many autistic adults still live with their parents; they don't want to move out or their parents are reluctant to let them try living on their own, or else they did let them try and it failed. In one case, an older brother denied me access.

Another girl explained to me that she didn't think that participating in this book would, for her, be a positive experience. She tried not to think about being autistic very often. All I got from one of my former classmates was a crackly phone call made, I think, from a booth; I think that he was trying to give me an address but he spoke very slowly, and I confused him by interrupting and asking for a number where I could call him back, and then there were beeps, he got cut off, and I never heard from him again. I'm afraid that, beyond this book, there may be a hinterland of autistic experience, remote and underformed.

'No, sir.'

Crucially, his daughter, Elizabeth, didn't get better. So much so that she committed suicide in 2002. I wanted to be allowed back into his house, I wanted him and his wife to talk more to me, because Elizabeth's story was important. I was in danger of turning her into an emblem of autistic misery, of making her stand for all those whom I didn't get to talk to, whose troubles I had to imagine (whose triumphs, though there will be some, I didn't dare to imagine), of sticking all those arrows in her flesh. I wanted to avoid this fate by learning more about her. It was worse because I didn't remember her. I had been told that we learnt to play the piano together. I had been told that sometimes my parents picked us both up and sometimes hers. But I didn't remember her. And I didn't have much to go on.

I had spoken to Elizabeth's father once before, over the telephone. All our subsequent contact, prior to my arrival in Los Angeles, had been by email. When we spoke, he apologized that the television was on in the background. It was on still, as we sat silently in his living-room. He explained, in that first conversation, that the television had always been kept on because Elizabeth made noises. She spoke better and better, with each year, but she still made noises. Whenever she became even slightly distressed, she made noises from the back of her throat. It was something that she couldn't control. So they left the television on, so that she didn't feel embarrassed about the noises, so that they weren't ever the only sound in the room.

A few days after this initial telephone conversation, I was coming home from work by the subway. My local underground station has lifts to bring you up from the bottom rather than escalators. At the back of the lift, that day, was a man, probably in his forties. He was smartly dressed but not properly so. His tie wasn't well-knotted. His trousers bunched up at the cuffs. He didn't like being in the lift. He shifted around. He kept his gaze on the floor. And he made noises from the back of his throat. I wanted to take his hand. I wanted to stand behind him and put my arms around him. I didn't, of course. And all the other passengers in the lift obviously felt uncomfortable. They willed the doors to shut quicker than they did, for the lift to climb quicker than it did, to leave him behind quicker than they were able to. I thought of Elizabeth intensely. I wanted to remember her and, failing that, to know more about her. I didn't want to think of her as a person in a lift, and other people's embarrassment at being around her.

There was a single photograph of Elizabeth on the mantelpiece at her parents' home in Los Angeles. She was wearing a cycle helmet, and an ice-blue sweatshirt, standing beside a tree. Her hair was in a ponytail. Incongruously, she looked like the sort of person who might start a conversation with you by way of rubbing your arm and asking, 'How are you, sweetie?'

Her father cleared his throat again.

'Tell me about the boy who has these puppets.'

So I did. And I began to think of the questions that I wanted to ask.

Elizabeth's father, Henry, led us towards the top of the Bunker Hill Steps. It was an evocative name, though the effect was ruined somewhat by the escalators that ran up alongside them. He explained that the steps were built recently to accompany One Bunker Hill, the first skyscraper in the West. Construction began in 1930, at the apex of the Great Depression, but the building was completed none-theless. It was also the first all-electrical building on this side of the continent. Henry spoke like a historian. He had a good line in sweeping arm motions. It didn't take long to climb to the top. When we got there, there was a pond, a fish restaurant, and the entrance to a car park. Henry paused to enjoy the look of befuddlement on my face.

'This is America, Kamran. The steps lead to places neither old nor specific.'

I nodded. 'There's some hills though,' I tried. They were visible past a tall brown building past the entrance to the car park.

'It's always possible to see hills in this city,' he replied. He headed off to the left. There were a number of buildings around us. I shaded my eyes and looked at each one in turn.

'Which is One Bunker Hill?' I asked.

He paused. 'It's the one you can't see,' he replied with some delight. It was only twelve stories high. Its spot on the

145

skyline had been nabbed by considerably taller buildings. Sheila, Elizabeth's mother, and I followed him off to the side into another garden. It was vaguely Oriental. Or, by shades, Italian. It was really difficult to say. It was owned by Citibank.

'Everything in LA belongs,' suggested Henry.

We walked through the garden and sat down around a table. It was a sunny and sweaty day. A week ago, schools nearby had been closed due to flood waters. I had noticed a sign on the sidewalk that cautioned against dumping into a crevice. 'Drains to ocean,' it explained. Across the road was the Los Angeles Central Library. At around our eye level, there was an inscription. It took me a large amount of time to realize that it wasn't in Latin, that, oddly, it was written in English. I read, 'Books alone are liberal and free. They give to all who ask. They emancipate all who serve them faith-fully.'

'Elizabeth liked to come here,' explained Henry.

After a pause, Sheila added, 'There were at least a couple of times that Elizabeth came here.'

The striking thing was not that she came, but that she came alone. Like around half of autistic adults, Elizabeth lived with her parents. There were a couple of spells during which she was taken into care – following a declaration by professionals that she was a danger to herself and that continuous professional supervision was needed to mitigate that danger – but, aside from that, she lived at home. Henry and Sheila wanted, though, for her to be able to do certain things alone, to have learnt them and to feel capable as a consequence.

First, they tried to negotiate with the local newsagent that she be given a delivery round. But he was afraid of losing trade. Then, they tried to teach her about gardening. But she grew terrified when dirt adhered to her clothes. She came rushing indoors, stripped, and insisted on entry to the shower. She was interested in the library, however. She liked the building – an almost orange stone, she wrote in her notebook, smaller than it liked to hope it was. She enjoyed walking around it, sitting in different parts of the gardens that surrounded it. When she visited it for the first time with them, she wrote down all the inscriptions from the façade in her notebook; Henry and Sheila both kept notebooks, a practice that they successfully transmitted to their daughter. They let me look through a stack of them. I found one where an entire Sesame Street episode had been transcribed verbatim, alternate lines in different inks, so presumably over the course of repeated viewings rather than just one; I found another containing reproductions of newspaper front-pages – these were careful sketches featuring spectacularly exact lettering. I didn't come across any notes on dreams, or accounts of things done. The books were more like logs than journals.

In order to teach her how to get from their home to the library, Henry and Sheila began by teaching Elizabeth the way to the nearest bus stop. The way that autistic people are normally taught new tasks is by breaking them down into sections. Two or three evenings a week, after dinner, one or both of them walked with her to the bus stop. They stood there for a while, watching buses stop or go past. They explained the numbers on the fronts of the buses, and the motions made by people waiting in order to catch the driver's attention. It is easy to understand why autistic people are often mistaken for being retarded. Elizabeth may not have realized, standing there on her own, that there was a correlation between people sticking out their hands and the bus pulling in. She may not have realized, not because she lacked deductive reasoning, but because she may have noticed the green stain on the person's sneakers instead, or the misplaced apostrophe in the advertisement on the side of the bus. She may have noticed that the old woman standing beside her had trim fingernails with the exception of her left thumb, but she may have missed her bus – what we consider to be the obvious hierarchy of sense data is not so obvious to everyone. And so, Henry and Sheila taught her what was relevant to her purpose.

The next step was teaching her when to get off the bus. They started ambitiously. They put up a street map and a bus map on the kitchen wall. Elizabeth needed to follow the green line and then the orange one, so Henry drew the lines from the bus map on to the street map, in green and orange marker. Since the bus map was stylized and simplified, he talked her through the differences. Elizabeth grew interested in this part and Henry got to tell her about subway maps too, which didn't accurately depict either the train lines or the relations between different parts of a city, but which were more useful because they were abstract.

Sheila and Elizabeth took their next trip with a portable copy of the same map. Henry drew the lines on to a smaller, fold-out version. But Elizabeth couldn't follow their route on it. Each time the bus stopped, Elizabeth thought that she was to count off a dot, except that the bus stopped for traffic lights and pedestrian crossings, as well as to pick up or let off passengers. And also, to make things worse, it didn't stop every time that it was supposed to. There weren't passengers to let off or pick up at every point designated on the map. So Elizabeth's tally of stops didn't match their progress on the map. Sheila tried to correct her mistakes and guide her finger over the lines but Elizabeth grew increasingly confused. She began to kick the seat in front of her. Sheila had to bring her off the bus. They sat down on the sidewalk until Elizabeth felt easier. They took a taxi home.

After that exercise, Henry and Sheila abandoned the bus map. It was confusing Elizabeth. She didn't understand that it was just a guide. She needed something more exact. She couldn't be expected to rely on her interpretation of whether the bus had stopped or whether it was a bus stop. The next strategy was to teach her to count streets, to use just the street map and to count the streets to her two destinations. However, when they tried this, she disputed their interpretation of a street. She wanted to count everything that was paved as a street. Again the map didn't match what she was seeing. They tried to wean her off this by telling her to count only those paved routes that had street signs. This had the potential for excluding entrances to parking garages and walkways. She was good at noticing details so it seemed safe to assume that she would notice every street sign and cross-reference them with the map. However, not every street on the map had a sign, far from it, especially when they got downtown. They also tried by counting only those that had white lines drawn on them. But some of the wider streets had several lanes – so several white lines – and some of the narrower streets had no lines. This didn't work either.

During another unsuccessful attempt, they had to get off the bus early again. Sheila ripped up their latest, annotated street map and threw it in the trash. Henry reached out to take her hand but she slapped it away. They'd been trying for three weeks by that point. The task had become the bane of their weekends. They'd always considered themselves to be resourceful. Their friends had too. Now they were having to explain their continuing failure. Blind people traveled on buses. Children did.

'Where are we anyway?' exclaimed Sheila.

'Twelve,' replied Elizabeth. She was holding a piece of string that she had tied into dozens of knots. She was trying not to get too anxious when the schemes didn't work so she had found a task to focus on.

'What?' asked Henry. 'Why twelve?'

Elizabeth pointed to the bus stop.

She had worked out that the bus map wasn't at all abstract. It was only abstract if you were comparing it to the street map, or if you assumed that the bus had to stop at every dot. Instead the bus map was a map of all the bus-stop signs with the same logo as was in the bottom right-hand corner of the map. In fact, you didn't even need the map. You just needed to know the number of signs from the point of embarkation to the point of disembarkation. They were at twelve. They needed to get to fifteen. Then they needed to transfer to the second bus and go to six. She had thought of it recently. It was the first trip on which she was trying to see if it worked. Sheila kissed her on the forehead and held her for a very long time.

'She was twenty-three years old,' added Henry. I had gone to the edge of the terraced garden, to look over the railing for the bus stop. Sheila came over and pointed it out to me. She turned back to her husband.

'Really, it was that long ago?'

*

It was difficult to think of Elizabeth being twenty-three, or older (she was twenty-six when she killed herself). It was difficult for me to think of her in a fixed way at all. I didn't remember her from New York. All that came into my head was the outline of a figure – a girl sitting at a piano – and now a girl on a bus, the two linked by the photograph on her parents' mantelpiece. André I had sitting on the steps outside the school, a red tie placed, not tied, around his neck. I had since then stayed with him. Also with Randall. Craig had come so far as to stay in my house. Elizabeth, though, was indistinct.

She left the school because neither Henry nor Sheila were happy in New York. They moved to California, where Sheila had been brought up. 'I missed the sunshine,' she explained. 'I am a serious person and yet I wanted there to be sunshine. A breakthrough in my research, social justice – of course – many other things, but also sunshine.' Elizabeth settled in well at first. Henry and Sheila found another school for her. The furniture was more colorful than in the one in New York, the teachers read fewer books on psychology and development, but it was fine. Elizabeth began to use signs to ask for things, a positive development; this was often the first stage in communication for individuals at the harsher end of the autism spectrum. Leaping straight to speech was ill-advised and rarely successful – any language learnt was entirely rote, prod-and-pinch techniques produced only a small set of words, and the opportunity for genuine development, while the brain was

151

still spongy, was compromised. It was important to illustrate more clearly to an autistic child the connection between the act of communication and the objective. Language was too abstract – the word 'melon' failed to resemble a melon and so it was no good to just learn the word without also learning that it wasn't supposed to resemble a melon, that the real point was, for example, to use the word in order to get a melon when you wanted one. Using signs was therefore better if full language teaching would be premature.

They also found a good piano teacher. Crucially, he was casual about his talent as a pianist. He enjoyed playing, thought that some other people should enjoy it too and hoped that a good portion of the remainder of persons enjoyed listening. But that was about all. If he hadn't been a pianist, he might have been the assistant manager of a mattress showroom, or a really good mechanic. This meant that he didn't put too much pressure on Elizabeth. There were still times when she groaned lightly sitting at the piano and, when she rested her hands, she often scrunched them into fists; however, she was soon able to turn to complex pieces of music and learnt relatively quickly how to play them through. She often played on her own and Henry and Sheila believed that this was a reasonable form of enclosure. Many other things were difficult. She had nasty psoriasis on her left leg for a year and had to wrap a dressing around it twice a day. There were a range of foods that she couldn't digest very well and the range seemed to be a shifting one. School was difficult. It left her tired. They felt therefore that it was important for her to have an activity that she could withdraw into, one that she was good at, and to which there was attached no embarrassment whatsoever.

One morning in the summer, they were sitting by their pool while Elizabeth was practicing indoors. Henry commented that he liked it when she practiced in the mornings. He didn't read a newspaper over breakfast. He preferred to emerge into the world slowly, after a swim, and a long shower. When Elizabeth played the piano first thing in the morning, he felt that they had this trait in common.

'Is she really practicing though?' asked Sheila. 'What is she practicing for?' Elizabeth was nine years old at the time. She was not too young to begin performing, to start giving recitals locally. Henry thought about this for a moment and then gripped the arms of the chair really tightly.

'I see what you mean,' he replied.

When she thought about why her daughter would never be able to perform, Sheila was skeptical about the importance of flair. After all, Elizabeth played what she was supposed to play and she would play it better and better as time went on. The compositions were incredibly exact. The timing was prescribed. Weren't the best performers the ones who got closest to the composition itself? Wasn't that why we thought Bach was a greater talent than anyone who played his music? Of course, performers added physical flourishes and their expressions changed between different passages of music, but that was all extraneous. It didn't matter if Elizabeth didn't do any of that; she could still play.

At the same time, though, Sheila knew that people would find it odd to watch someone who gave no response of her own to the music. She might argue that this gave them more scope to find their own response, but live performance, plainly, was about responding to the person as well as the music that she played. Spectating was impure and greedy in exactly that way.

Her worry was broadened by the likelihood that Elizabeth would find it very difficult to perform in combination with others. Playing the piano was a form of local coherence. This might mean that she would be untousled about playing in front of other people – she wouldn't be performing, she'd be playing her piano. She might be in her bedroom, she might be in an auditorium, it wouldn't make any difference – but playing with other people would be challenging. She would need to do something other than follow the score, for there may be mistakes, or quirks, in what the others played.

What it came down to was that playing alone would be simplest but she'd be unlikely to be successful as people looked for flair in soloists. She could be an accompanist – she'd seem a very generous one, she wouldn't seek the attention of the audience in any way – but she may not be any good at it.

Henry and Sheila sat silently until Elizabeth played through to the end of the piece of music. Then Sheila went indoors, rang the piano teacher, and reduced the frequency of the lessons to once a week.

*

It was typically Sheila who initiated these conceptual advances. Henry preferred to leave things to bob up to the surface on their own. Either that, or he simply relied on Sheila to ask these questions and was glad that she was willing to. Sheila, for her part, liked to take parenting as seriously as this. She often made notes to help her figure things out. And she didn't mind that her hopes for her daughter underwent a contraction from time to time. The reason for having a child had never been to turn her into a great pianist or a ballerina or a doctor. The only thing that Sheila was sore about was that her daughter would never become an equal, never someone who would challenge her. Instead, her role as a mother was to take as much of what she already knew or believed and make it as accessible as possible to Elizabeth. Having an autistic daughter meant that she really was in the business of reproduction and she had never wanted to be.

Henry took a less pessimistic view. He liked to bring home stories about colleagues whom he was pretty sure were autistic. He had always gotten excited about computer technology but now it also bore the promise that Elizabeth could work from home. She needn't be limited by her inability to live away from her parents, to commute easily on her own, or to manage relationships in a workplace. So it was Henry who was cut open when Elizabeth developed epilepsy. He was with her when the first attack took place.

He had decided to take her to a conference with him in New York. He wanted to stand with her on top of the Empire State Building. He wanted to go to Ellis Island with her and show her the names of her ancestors in the registers of immigrants that were displayed there. She was twelve. Her language development had picked up. As had her tantrums. Autistic children tend to withdraw when they feel frustrated. They try to do something soothing, or easier, that doesn't involve other people. They like to hide. Or rock. Elizabeth liked to rub crayon on the walls of her bedroom, vigorously to begin with, slowing as her panic subsided. Often, as autistic individuals grow older, as the frustrations are repeated, resentment develops. Sometimes this is directed at themselves, sometimes at the people – usually the parents – who, unwittingly, despite their best efforts, are responsible for the frustrating experiences. I used to throw tantrums. I once peeled a strip of wallpaper from the living-room that my father had just finished decorating, leaving a stripe of pale insolence running across the room, all because he had tidied away my toy cars, which he needed to do to avoid getting paint on them, but which had been parked against the skirting board in exactly the order that I wanted. Elizabeth hit both her parents. She smashed things. And Henry thought that he had caused another tantrum when, on the flight from Los Angeles to New York, he compelled her to stow her tray table as the plane began its descent.

It was only when another passenger from across the aisle exclaimed loudly that he began to realize that there was a different explanation for what Elizabeth was doing. That passenger suffered from epilepsy herself; she took charge, an air steward helped, and Henry stroked his daughter's head until they landed and proper medical attention was rushed on to the plane. Suddenly there were more precautions to learn, more practiced explanations from medical professionals to absorb and, even so, Elizabeth seemed to recede further from their ken. Henry missed the conference; he didn't give his paper; they didn't ask him to contribute a chapter to the book. But none of this mattered – though Sheila assured him that it was allowed to – and what he thought about instead was that there were already so many limits that his daughter had to negotiate, and it was possible that there were now too many.

Over the following months, she looked like she had been beaten up, or that she was having bad dreams, dreams so disturbing that she was afraid to talk about them. Sometimes she cried openly, which she had never done before. On the other hand, she began to say 'yes' more often. She'd go with them on walks and to restaurants, she'd try on clothes, help them pick furniture. She seemed to understand that they were under greater strain and, realizing this, they almost felt worse on seeing the efforts that she made to make them feel better. The three of them were approaching an impasse, where by trying to take better care of each other, they ran the risk of mutely watching television every evening, because any conversation or any activity might shift the balance of concern. If, for example, Henry and Sheila tried to pick Elizabeth's favourite activities, she might, for their sake, pretend to enjoy them more than she was doing, and they would then feel bad for her having to do so. Henry began taking antidepressants for the first time in his life. Sheila found them, frowned at him very hard, and showed him her own.

It was Sheila, again, who made a radical decision. She found a camp that was just for young autistic adults. Aged fourteen, Elizabeth was going to be one of the youngest there but the fortnight was well-structured and the staff seemed capable. Sheila checked a map – the site was close, within a two-hour drive. And so she convinced Henry that they should let Elizabeth go.

It didn't go well. They got a phone call on the third day. Elizabeth had fallen, broken two ribs, and punctured her left lung. They drove to the hospital immediately. Sheila left Henry to park the car and ran into the ward. She needed to know urgently and as soon as Elizabeth looked up to note her arrival, she did; her daughter hadn't really fallen, close enough, but not really. She wanted to slap her. She wanted to pull the bed off the wall and hurl it down the corridor. Instead, she kicked Elizabeth's slippers, sat down and composed herself for her husband's arrival.

Elizabeth stayed off school for three months after that. Henry and Sheila each began spending one day a week at home. On the days that they weren't there, Sheila required Elizabeth to ring her office every two hours. If she ever missed a phone call, one of them would rush home as soon as possible. But they never rang her in between those calls. They also hired a psychologist for her to talk to twice a week. They wanted her to have an emotional life that was separate from theirs and, within their duty of care, they still took the boldest steps that they could think of to help her in that cause.

Psychologists find it difficult to help autistic individuals for a variety of reasons. Craig and I both saw psychologists throughout our teens but we were relatively high-functioning and, though our autism was the primary reason why we were referred to psychologists, being autistic also meant that we were already thinking harder than most teenagers about how we related to other people and why we acted the way that we did. Being autistic meant that we had to be more deliberate in these matters anyway; talking to a psychologist often felt like a duplication of effort. First we'd have to bring this person up to date on our own thoughts and then watch them fumble towards an answer, though we already had one of our own. Also, because we were smart, and very aware of being smart, in an irritating clever-boy-good-with-numbers-and-long-words sort of way, we were rarely convinced that their answers were any better than our own.

I wasted a lot of my parents' money by stretching out contests of wills with my psychologists. I told them that I had learnt that I was adopted. Every time I invented a dream, it ended with the psychologist standing naked at the foot of my bed. I thanked them at the end of each session with gleaming unction. I was a brat. Those conversations did, however, form a view that I probably still hold – I hardly believe that others can provide emotional succour. I regard talking about my emotions as primarily a rhetorical exercise. Or an important act of reciprocation – if I don't from time to time talk about my emotions, others might stop talking to me about theirs and then I would feel dreadful, that I'd forced them to shut up. Whenever I do reveal sadness, even if it is to the extent of tears, I feel swiftly that I am manipulating the other person and that I must stop. It's an unhelpful set of traits, but I think it flows from the feeling that I can't properly access the feelings of others and so how can they access mine?

Elizabeth's relationship with her psychologist was different. Her psychologist was a creep. Autistic individuals often impel sympathy. Other people want to protect them, to care for them; it is remarkable, for example, how often even clinicians mention that autistic children have beautiful eyes. Elizabeth's psychologist wanted to wrap her in silk thread and keep her in his loft. He encouraged her to cherish her sadness. He told her not to make too many friends, to tell him things before she told them to her parents. So this was a difficult time for Elizabeth. She was the cynosure of other people's designs. Her parents and her teachers were cautious, at least, wary of exercising heteronomy; her psychologist plainly was not.

She spent a lot of time on her own though, as well. And, in secret, she taught herself how to ride a bicycle. There was an old woman, living on the same street, who rode her bicycle every day. From her bedroom, Elizabeth could see a large portion of her route. Sheila still kept a bicycle. It was in the garage and infrequently used. Elizabeth had hitherto thought of it as an adult object. For a long time, it had been taller than her. The spokes looked like they would transmit a shock if she touched them. It was almost as if, to make it work, she needed to be attached to it in some way.

She began by propping it up off the wall of the garage and learning how to get on and off it. She noticed that this was difficult and that even the neighbor who rode every day often stumbled; she had fallen a couple of times and Elizabeth, even watching from a distance, had felt dizzy. Elizabeth sometimes struggled for balance, especially in the mornings. She had developed the habit of rolling out of bed, literally, like a commando darting for cover, to avoid standing up immediately and feeling her head spin. Her father had bought her a key-ring with a compass in it once, and dizziness felt like the moment when she took the ring out of her pocket and the arrow bobbed about looking for North, except speeded up.

Once she could mount and dismount the bicycle, she began to wheel it to the end of the driveway and then back again. She did this as if she were running with the bicycle between her legs. She got very good at this and could do it very quickly − it was enough for a while. But then some younger children saw her riding the bicycle this way and laughed and she decided anew to learn to do it properly.

Throughout this period, she was meticulous about making the phone calls to her mother − every two hours. She also stopped wearing skirts and shorts because there were grazes on her knees and shins. She didn't explain this to her parents. They noticed but decided that it was a bad idea to make an issue out of what she wore and so said nothing about it.

They only learnt that she was riding a bicycle when, one morning, Sheila returned home to retrieve some examination scripts that she had left behind. She braked to a halt, out of what may have been horror or delight or doubt about her eyesight, when she saw Elizabeth turn into their street ahead of her. Sheila got out of the car and stood at the top of the street for fifteen minutes watching Elizabeth do circuits of the cul-de-sac in which their house was situated before turning into their driveway. Sheila walked in the rest of the way and into the living-room where Elizabeth had just dialled her mother's office phone number to log in for the first time that morning. Elizabeth hurriedly put the phone down and Sheila, instantaneously, decided not to admit that she had seen her riding the bicycle. She explained about the examination scripts, fetched them, and left again. She cried all the way back to the car and then to campus; happier, happier than she had been for a long time.

After she told Henry, he waited three months and then bought two more bicycles. One evening, after dinner, he loaded them into a small trailer and hitched it to the car. Elizabeth came outside to watch what he was doing and began smiling. They all drove to a park and rode their bicycles for an hour. They began doing this from time to time. After the second time, when they were loading the bicycles back into the trailer, Elizabeth told them about how and when she had taught herself to ride. Sheila made her own confession and they ate ice cream on the way home. Henry explained that they wanted never to assume that she was inert but that, equally, they didn't want to swallow all of her accomplishments. He spoke at some length and Elizabeth looked puzzled, until she caught her mother's eye; Sheila began giggling and Elizabeth did too.

Neither Henry nor Sheila were afraid of depression. They expected it, not like a fall in the snow, but possibly in the way of a letter explaining that their tax return was mistaken and that they owed a little more money. In terms of tangible evidence, there was a record of alcoholism in Henry's family and Sheila's maternal grandmother had drowned in unlikely circumstances at the age of fifty. More than this, though, they both hefted around with them an enduring belief that happiness was not easy. They both had resources to mitigate depression, however. They had their work, which was often an alternative source of value. They read a lot of novels. They could talk most things through with one another. They worried about Elizabeth because they were afraid that she would simply be baffled by depression, that she wouldn't know what to do when she didn't want to get out of bed in the morning, when the sun rose only to disappear behind the clouds after a moment. She hadn't read about that feeling in books, and she couldn't learn as much from observing her family members, including her parents, suffer under the same mood.

And so it was; they were right about this. When depression struck, Elizabeth strained for traction. The panic developed fast. Sometimes she gasped, as if someone had grabbed hold of her leg, was pulling her down, and she needed a complete lungful of air to stand any chance of getting back up to the surface. The doctors were reluctant to put her on antidepressants or make any firm diagnosis of the malaise, partly because she was still a teenager, and partly because, well, wasn't it all really down to her autism?

Henry and Sheila disagreed. That she was sleeping badly wasn't due to autism. That the bags under her eyes were so heavy that they looked mouldy wasn't due to autism. Before, she may have spent a lot of her time in seclusion but she tried more frequently to engage, she drew herself up to her full height. Now she was becoming obstinate about not going to school. She was beginning to eschew the more difficult forms of local coherence. She hardly ever played the piano. She read less. She came down the stairs in the way that she had done since she was little – one at a time, on her backside – more often, sometimes over and over again for a couple of hours.

Then she put a syringe in her ankle. Henry had been diagnosed with diabetes and there were syringes in the bathroom cabinet, which they had never regarded as dangerous – Elizabeth couldn't even watch Henry administer his daily insulin shot. But, one evening, she called out and Sheila found her sitting at the top of the stairs. She had stuck the syringe in a long way. Sheila was afraid of breaking the needle if she tried to pluck it out, so they called their doctor who lived nearby but who then made them talk about it with Elizabeth's specialist. The specialist's worry was that Elizabeth had discovered something that night that she may explore further. He too was right.

Shortly thereafter, Henry and Sheila were told that their daughter was schizophrenic, or manic depressive; they were asked, separately, whether they had abused her sexually as a child. No doubt Elizabeth was asked about this more often. She was moved into a nearby residential clinic for young adults with similar notes on their medical records, who had been discovered making similar explorations into what they could withstand.

Henry and Sheila refused to set out the itinerary of the next five years. They also told me that they hadn't kept any letters from doctors. They offered me three scenes only.

The Hollander. They visited Elizabeth after three days. They sat down in the living area. Sheila counted off the pot plants that she could identify, Henry retied his shoelaces. The staff member who had led them in – with the inappropriate air, they thought, of a curator or the madam of a burlesque house – asked if they wanted some coffee. They both refused. Elizabeth came in a few minutes later. She was brought in by 'The Hollander'. Petra Hollander had been there for two years, she was around the same age as Elizabeth, and they had two other contemporaries too. Whenever someone came to see one of them, they linked hands to form 'The Hollander' and walked over to the guests together. The girl being visited was then allowed to decouple from the chain and the others continued walking.

On the one hand, Henry and Sheila were alarmed by this, it seemed to extend the 'House of the Rising Sun' metaphor. On the other hand, they suddenly realized that it was possible that Elizabeth wasn't going to be kept in a straitjacket, that the place might in fact have adequate heating, and that her closest companion need not be an old woman who thought that the Civil War was ongoing and kept a pet muskrat. They were surprised, with some force, that these were their unspoken expectations. For a while afterwards, they were thrown – were they supposed to struggle to get her out of the care system or were they supposed to be relieved that she was under the supervision of professionals and with other people her age? Elizabeth had never had close friends, who might understand better than they could how she felt in the mornings or what she saw when she looked in the mirror.

Chicago-style pizza. They were on a family trip. They had Elizabeth for three weeks and they could both spare to be out of Los Angeles, so they booked a series of flights and hotel rooms. While they were in Chicago, Elizabeth asked to eat Chicago-style pizza. Chicago-style pizza is stuffed, as well as topped, with ingredients. Elizabeth had heard about it from another of the patients. They took a restaurant re-commendation from their hotel concierge and stayed a long time. There were televisions up on the walls and a basketball game that Henry had wanted to watch. Elizabeth was attentive to her father's explanations. She asked questions about the records of the two teams on offensive rebounds and three-point shots. Sheila tried to work out whether she was feigning interest in order to please her father, which would be an impressive act of empathy for an autistic individual, or whether the game appealed to her, which was fine, but less significant for the purpose of putting together a story about her progress – something that Sheila and Henry had both inevitably been doing during the entire trip, discussing their latest drafts over breakfast in hotel dining-rooms after Elizabeth asked for a little longer in bed.

That night at the pizza restaurant, when a waiter started collecting condiments and shakers of Parmesan cheese from the empty tables, Elizabeth took theirs and put them in the corner, as if out of his reach. She put down her knife and fork after every three mouthfuls and wiped all her fingers on a napkin that she kept beside her plate. But it wasn't just this tableside behavior that suggested anxiety. Throughout their

165

trip, Elizabeth remained tense, or watchful; she didn't feel entirely safe. In anticipation of take-off and landing on each of their flights, she put her feet up against the seat in front of her and placed her hands on her forehead. It had never been proven that her first epileptic seizure was triggered by the change in air pressure as the plane began its descent – the same event had never again had the same consequence – but it was a theory that one doctor, albeit one out of many, had mentioned and she took it seriously and had devised this response. Still, she was sleeping better and eating more. She read the magazine on each flight – though nothing else – and rarely did she spend so long in the bathroom as to require Henry or Sheila to worry and listen at the door.

Towards the end of their dinner of Chicago-style pizza, they saw her collection of tablets for the first time. She had taken to carrying a small bag with her perenially. They had bought it for her, it was red and shaped like a flower. They hadn't thought hard about what she kept in it but assumed that it was her medicines plus some personal effects. She emptied it at the end of their meal and they discovered that it was all medicines. She began clicking off tops and counting out her doses. The tablets were different colors and different shapes. As the collection grew, it looked like it should be under glass in a museum. She asked to borrow the remainder of Henry's glass of water and began to work her way through her assortment, column by column. She explained that there was a column of capsules, one of tablets, and the third one was optional – they were all nutritional supplements – but she took them anyway. They didn't know what else to ask her. They were amazed that she had shown them. Then the waiter came to find out whether they wanted the rest of the pizza in a box to take away with them and Elizabeth nodded.

Fair-weather fans. Elizabeth learnt or read this phrase somewhere and began using it frequently for a few months. Henry and Sheila noticed it when they visited or took her out for a meal or to an event. If Henry failed to get a taxi to stop, for example, Elizabeth might say, while looking in the direction of the departing taxi, 'Fair-weather fan'. She used the phrase too often, but she timed her use of it well; when she was younger, she would have simply repeated it without meaning, much as Craig proclaimed, 'Send in the Idiots.' One afternoon, she was shopping for clothes with her mother and, after seeing two young men smoking together, she remarked, 'Fair-weather fans'. Sheila asked her why. Elizabeth didn't reply immediately, but then pulled up her left sleeve and showed her mother where she had burnt herself with a cigarette. Sheila swallowed her alarm.

'Why did you do that?' she asked pleasantly.

Again, Elizabeth didn't reply immediately. 'I did it a long time ago,' she remarked, after about a minute. 'I don't remember why I did it.'

'I did it once,' explained Sheila. 'The mark doesn't really go away.' She stopped and pulled up a trouser leg to show her.

'Why did you do that?' asked Elizabeth, using her mother's words − not to mock her, but probably because her mother had used them and so she recognized that they were the right ones.

'I wrote about it. I used to keep a diary then. Would you like to see it?'

Elizabeth nodded, and when she went back to the center,

she took with her two years' worth of her mother's diaries. Sheila had only wanted to give her a few pages, the ones relevant to the marks that they had compared, but Elizabeth had asked for more. Sheila worried about this intensely as soon as Elizabeth had gone. She hadn't wanted to deny her, but might the diaries make her feel that she was locked into a generational cycle, that she wouldn't emerge from it, only progress to the next phase? That meant she'd need to evaluate her mother's life and decide whether it was worth waiting for it. Would she think that it was? Was she now able to think like this at all? Sheila talked to Henry that night, confessed what she had done, and he announced, immediately, that this was right; while of course they had to keep balancing her safety against the value of a fuller life, they were in danger of adhering too firmly to the former and he was glad, really glad, that she had given Elizabeth the diaries. He then asked for more examples of when Elizabeth had said 'fair-weather fans' and laughed at each one.

*

Henry and Sheila told me these three stories after a violin concert at the Walt Disney Centre in downtown LA. It's a Frank Gehry building, shiny and startling. I kept expecting to see police cars and fire engines gathered around it and men with walkie-talkies trying to work out how it got there and what to do next. We walked around the building before the concert and we spoke about it; we touched it, stood in different places, tried to explain it. My mother was fond of commenting that most people spend most of their time thinking about the past or the future and that it is only a few people who think properly about the present. Henry and Sheila, I realized, were people who concentrated quite hard on the present. We spoke about the concert hall once we were inside, the design of the organ, the acoustics, how odd it was to watch a performance by a solo violinist – it was so unlike a performance. It was exciting to be with people who took the present seriously and, for Elizabeth, it must have been essential. Henry and Sheila paid attention. They didn't enclose themselves in a story about how unfair it was, or what their daughter must achieve; they engaged with what happened.

After the concert, we sat for a long time with cups of coffee. I told them my mother's view. Sheila shrugged her shoulders and Henry nodded. They weren't impressed with themselves; they did what they thought they should do. I asked Henry about what he had asked me when we first met: 'Why did you get better?'

'You didn't mean why did you get better and my daughter didn't?' I suggested.

'Elizabeth did get better.'

Henry nodded. He traced a line across his brow with the index finger on his right hand and then scratched his beard. 'Not a lot was expected of her when she was little. She did a lot of things. She learnt a lot of things.'

'Why did you ask me?'

'I wanted to know how you thought about autism. It was a quick way to find out.'

'Also, you were drunk,' added Sheila.

'Also, I was drunk,' admitted Henry. 'First time in a long while.'

The rigor with which Henry and Sheila liked to approach all things reminded me of my parents – for example, they too tended to claim the right to interview other people and other

169

people tended to acquiesce. Henry's question was high-stakes because I was planning to write about his daughter, but I think that he may have put it to me even if he had met me at a dinner party and he knew nothing about the topic beforehand; he would have wanted to work out how I, and other people who wrote about the condition, thought about it. He and Sheila, and my parents too, lived in a state of constant inquiry.

It was a good state to be brought up in. It meant that my first experiences of talking expansively were on topics of politics and culture around the dinner table. We always ate dinner properly, around a table – my parents, my sister and I – all absences had to be notified in advance. Perhaps it was best that talking to my parents meant talking about these things; I suspect that if they had pressed me to talk about feelings or what I did in my room alone, mumbling brief answers, I would only have disappointed them and that would have caused me to withdraw even more.

Their approach also meant that I had a lot of independence. Though my views on nuclear non-proliferation were tested at an early age, I was allowed to spend long evenings in my room on my own, free from benevolent though intrusive knocks at the door and offers of cocoa. Neither my sister nor I were ever given bedtimes and, from the age of six, getting up for school was our own responsibility. One morning when I was nine years old, I woke at the regular time, ate breakfast with my parents and then announced that I was going into the back garden to read a book rather than leave for school. They didn't question me until the evening and, then, all they checked was that I wasn't sick and that I wasn't being bullied. I was at a mainstream school by this stage. I assured them that there was nothing to worry about on either count; I just hadn't felt like going to school and had kept up with the class by working for a couple of hours in the afternoon. This continued for three days and, though they kept checking about my health, and no doubt they fielded calls from the school, they exerted no other pressure. On the fourth day, I ate breakfast, picked up my satchel and got on the school bus with my sister. And they asked no questions about this change of heart either.

It was only on spending time with Henry and Sheila and listening to their stories about Elizabeth that I properly realized how difficult it must have been for my parents to give me this independence. There must always have been the temptation to intervene, to disentangle things for this child of theirs who had been diagnosed with autism, who was shy though bright, odd though not really freaky. I did decide to stay at home for college but that was my decision and it always felt like my decision – my parents were exceptionally enthusiastic about bringing me on college visits, both in the US and the UK. Their enthusiasm for these visits and for ordering prospectuses was such that I almost felt, from time to time, that they would prefer me to go to college elsewhere. I now know that this wasn't the case, that they were scared stiff that I might go to college somewhere faraway – this wasn't only because of the remains of my autism, it was also because I was only sixteen and everyone else there would be at least one, and usually two, years older than me. I now know that it was only after several prolonged and careful discussions, with courage, that they decided to leave it to me. Though I've now lived away from home for over six years, they still call me four or five times a week. They ask very little, they don't pry, but it's important to them that we speak so regularly – it's the compromise between the enhanced duty of care that they feel and their desire and their joy that I have my independence.

As a waitress cleared our coffee cups away, Henry and Sheila told me that they still thought about Elizabeth a lot. They missed her. She remained an important part of their lives, except now she couldn't change and she couldn't ever surprise them. Henry described how sometimes, when he was browsing for books, or when he sat at his desk and found himself staring out of the window, or when he went into the trees to find a golf ball that he had mishit and forgot why he had gone there, it would suddenly feel like someone had passed behind him and tapped him on the shoulder, and only then did he realize that he was thinking of her and the ground quivered for an instant. Sheila sometimes felt that she was being asked to jump from the roof of one building to the next and, though the jump looked possible, as soon as she leapt, she realized that the gap was too large.

Eventually they told me about the day that she died. I almost didn't want them to, by then, but I think that we all knew that it was unavoidable. Elizabeth had been living at home again for close to two years. She took fewer pills but still enough to need two separate pillboxes should she, or they, be going out for more than a few hours. She felt panicky relatively often. She felt like a jug of coffee, she said, like her body was giving off steam, that it was syrupy inside; her head became full of black and red and indigo. She sometimes needed to grab hold of things because she felt like either she would slide backwards if she didn't or the object would slide towards her and trap her. She played the piano from time to time; whenever she did, she played for hours. She also began to give piano lessons, first to a neighbor's child – the family had moved in not long ago, and the father heard her play one evening while he was visiting. The child hadn't played before and so Elizabeth guided her through the initial exercises, stood her on a chair and explained how the insides of the piano worked. This phase was successful, and the child learnt well. So Henry and Sheila mentioned the idea to some of their colleagues and friends and soon Elizabeth was teaching six or seven hours a week. They never organized the sessions themselves. They always put the parents of the child in touch directly with Elizabeth. Sheila sometimes made the telephone call when a lesson had to be canceled, when Elizabeth didn't feel able to give the lesson, but otherwise Elizabeth kept a diary and a list of telephone numbers. The only difficulty was that she wasn't necessarily patient. She became confused when a student became confused. Sometimes they stared at one another fiercely, or huffily looked away from one another, like friends disagreeing in the school playground at lunchtime. Once she shouted at an eight-year-old; another time, she threw her copy of the music at a nine-year-old. Nothing came of it – the children didn't tell their parents; they were all very fond of Elizabeth – but Henry and Sheila worried about it and, whenever they were home during a lesson, they listened at the door from time to time.

There was no cataclysmic event that triggered her suicide. There was no portentous statement made in the days leading up to it. She left no note. The toxicology report showed a combination of drugs in her system. She had swallowed the contents of most of her bottles and jars, even the nutritional supplements. She had done it in the bathroom, which was where they were kept, in a large cabinet with a mirror door. She then went downstairs and peeled back a corner of the tarpaulin that was covering the swimming pool during the winter and climbed into the water amid the rotting leaves and gulch.

It was a Sunday morning and both Sheila and Henry were at home. They didn't know how long she was in the pool before Sheila noticed that the cover had been moved aside. She went outside to see what had happened. She said that she had no foreboding of it. Her womb did not wobble momentarily, she did not think of the infant at her breast – all that was nonsense. She saw her daughter in the pool and she screamed.

Henry was upstairs in his study when he heard his wife scream. He can't remember thinking anything specific; all he remembers is hearing the scream and then getting up from his seat and hurrying down the stairs. He doesn't remember the time in between those two events. By the time he arrived by the pool, Sheila had pulled Elizabeth out of the water; she had called an ambulance, it had come, the paramedic had rubbed his eyes and told Sheila that her daughter was dead. Sheila lay down beside Elizabeth and put her arm around her. That was how Henry found them. The ambulance staff didn't know what to do, whether to ask Sheila to move, whether to leave and come back later, which procedurally they couldn't do though it seemed right.

Henry shuddered as he told me this part.

'It is my regret,' he said. 'I should have liked to help my wife pull Elizabeth out of the water. I don't know what happened to me.' Sheila rubbed his arm, between shoulder

174

and elbow. She posed her other arm in a bodybuilding way and then pointed to her bicep. Henry and I smiled, grateful for what she was trying to do. Later, while Sheila had gone to the bathroom, Henry told me that he removed the medicine cabinet as soon as they came back from the hospital. He imagined that his daughter had looked at herself in the mirror after each swig of tablets and he couldn't bear to have that thought every time he used the mirror to shave or to comb his hair.

We parted shortly thereafter that evening. The next day they took me on a tour of Hollywood and Universal City. They thought these places were extremely funny and they wanted me to share the joke. It was exciting, spending the day with them, these serious people who liked detail, who liked to notice things, who stopped for coffee or a meal roughly every two hours and talked furiously at one another. Their intelligence could consume anything, I supposed, or sustain it. I think that Elizabeth got better because of them, because of their attention, because they didn't panic. I haven't met people like them very often. I am amazed that they are not assailed more often by regret, or desperation, but I am glad that they are not.

The last thing that they said to me before I left Los Angeles was, 'Don't come back here.'

I paused, staring at them as if the set of their faces might reveal the tone in which the statement was made. It didn't. 'What do you mean?' I had to ask.

'Make us visit London,' they smiled.

I nodded vigorously.

5

HER OFFICE WAS LINED with red carpet. When I first knew Ira, I frequently paid closer attention to the carpet than to her. I preferred to sit on the carpet rather than in any of the chairs that were available. I could change the shade of the carpet by brushing my hand over it. I could draw pictures in it by manipulating the pile with my fingers. Often I had to explain what the pictures were of – as if it wasn't obvious.

Ira sat behind her desk, in a large chair that looked like an arcade machine. Whenever she clambered out of it, she seemed to become smaller, as if she passed through a glass screen. Sometimes she came over and sat down next to me on the carpet. This wasn't easy for her; I remember that she had to fold herself into a sitting position and that she had to shift regularly. I remember that she wore shoes with heels. Her hair smelt almost the same as my mother's.

She did a variety of exercises with me. We listened to tapes of a couple named Tom and Maureen. I had to identify the topics of their conversation. I had to ascribe to them motives and emotional states. For example, how did Maureen's voice sound when Tom said that their daughter wasn't going to visit at the weekend? Could I describe it? Ira also held up cards with words on them and I had to guess what the next word was. During these exercises, I sometimes broke off and went back to drawing pictures in the carpet. I shook my head when she challenged me. I shrugged and mumbled, 'I've run out of words.'

Ira and I had a contest once to find the best description of how I felt when the words ran out. She wondered if it was like going into the labyrinth to fight the minotaur only to find that the ball of string wasn't long enough. I suggested no, it was more like walking along a tightrope only to discover halfway through that your laces were untied.

We had this contest again when we met twenty years later in New York. I knew from the beginning that, though my primary aim was to trace my former classmates, I also needed to meet our teachers. They were part of what my classmates and I had in common. Some of the others had had Ira's red-carpet treatment too. Certainly we'd all sat in Ms. Russell's circle listening to her read the newspaper. It was also, I think, that I wanted to take my findings to them and learn what they thought of what their former students had and had not managed to do – my observations were one thing, but theirs would be more objective, better grounded, with a keener and fuller sense of what we were like as children and how children with autism typically developed.

It had been so long since I had seen Ira that there was no prospect we would recognize one another. She told me beforehand that she would adopt a big green scarf as a visual aid. I spotted it at an outside table from across the street. She was wearing it with a camel-colored trouser suit. As I got closer, I realized that I didn't know how to start a conversation with her. I was a child when I knew her before; she was already an adult then, already an adult clinician working with autistic and other children for close to ten years. I had turned into an adult too but she might have referred to her twenty-year-old case-notes on me before she came out to meet me; from what I guessed of her, she wasn't the sort of person who threw away old papers – she might have read them on the subway, she might have them in her bag which was lying by her feet.

I took a deep breath and sat down. I immediately began to meddle with the small vase that was set on the right-hand side of the table. She took off her scarf and arranged it around the back of her chair. A waitress provided two glasses of water and I wiped a stripe of condensation from the outside of mine. I knew that Ms. Russell – or Rebecca, as I was now able to call her – was due to join us; how soon would she come? I squirmed out of my jacket and watched a car turn into the street that ran alongside the café.

I had thought about this meeting a lot. I had planned to explain that I had listened to the tape of Tom and Maureen again recently and that the interesting thing about Tom and Maureen was that they were unhappy with one another, that they probably slept in separate beds, that they had completely different friends. I thought that this would be a funny opening and that it would show how much sharper my insight into other people's feelings had become. It was also an odd opening though. Did I want to be rediagnosed?

Finally, she smiled.

'Hello, Kamran,' she said.

'I didn't time the silence,' I replied, 'but it was long.'

She nodded but added nothing more. I tried not to grimace. This meeting was already nerve-racking.

What I had found in talking to the Idiots about our former teachers was that none of us remembered Ira as well as Rebecca. Ira was the director of the school. We remembered her walking down corridors, talking to our parents, tapping her right foot against the ground as she did so; we remembered that she sat in a chair that looked like an arcade machine. But this was about all. I remembered her a little better than the others as I'd spent more time with her, but I felt that I had to scuttle around to find my recollections; they hadn't adhered to one another.

This haziness bothered me. It came on top of realizing that I had no memory of Elizabeth at all. Perhaps I should speak to Ira about this to start off with. I knew that the philosopher Daniel C. Dennett believed that acquiring a language is a *necessary precondition* for consciousness. Although pre-linguistic children may stare intently, grasp at most things that they can reach, although they will yelp if they are hurt, they are not conscious. There is no subject to gather these sensory data, to turn them into experiences. There is merely a cerebral locus of effects. As Dennett argues it, as the ability to talk develops, so do further abilities. The mind becomes able to review, to muse, to rehearse, recollect, and, in general, engage events occurring in the nervous system. Hitherto, these have purely, and, with babies, often literally, hand-to-mouth effects. Signals and motor responses bounce around leaving no memories in their wake. Obviously Dennett couldn't prove this, but did I begin to make out his case? I retained hardly any details at all from the time when my language abilities were too limited to engage the stuff of the world around me.

Abruptly, I realized that Ira and I had now spent some more time without saying anything to one another. I had forgotten to use my gambit about Tom and Maureen.

'Do you still play tapes of Tom and Maureen?' I asked plainly, my confidence to use the more expansive version of my question now eviscerated.

Ira shook her head. She started telling me about a computer program that she used instead. It was called 'Ultimate Learning Fun with Feelings'. Level 1 of the program starts by introducing the child to around twenty different emotions in the form of cartoons. On Level 2, the user – Ira tapped the table as she said the word 'user' – learns the facial and body features that correspond to each emotion learned in Level 1. For example, a picture of a happy person smiling is shown with a question: 'You can tell this person is happy because?' The user is asked to select an answer from the choices given. The correct answer in this case is, 'The mouth is going up.' Then the program begins to add layers of complexity. Level 3 demonstrates how events can cause emotions. Typical examples include: 'The boy is happy because he got a birthday present,' and 'The girl is sad because her bike is broken.' Level 4 proceeds to teach the verbal aspects of these emotions. On this level, voices are played and the user has to match them to the picture of the corresponding emotion, choosing the right one from a range of options. Level 5 begins to put the various 'learnings' – another tap on the table – to the test. There are videos of actors demonstrating the range of emotional states covered by the program. Applying the range of criteria learnt from Levels 1–4, the user is asked to identify the emotional state of the person in the video.

Then there is a final challenge. Level 6 features a crowded room and the child, or the user, aims to ascribe to each person in the crowd one specific emotional state. According to the software company's website, which I looked at later, 'After successful completion of Level 6, the user is ready for real world, appropriate communication and interaction.' Ira explained that it was a useful piece of software in spite of the sales material, which could be a little doctrinaire. I also found on the website the following statement:

Coupled with poor conversational skills, the autistic child is doomed to a life of isolation without a chance for developing significant relationships in the social world. In the absence of a cure for autism through some magic bullet, we must rely on learning and behavior modification to teach the special needs child how to assess the emotional states of others. Since the data used for this process may be overwhelming, a method that breaks down the individual components of an emotion is necessary.

This could have been written better – though what I mean is that I found it hard to read, given its claim that autism would prove to be my doom. However, there was strong evidence that early and intensive training of this sort could have dramatic results. Though autism was probably a neurobiological disorder at heart, the primary interventions were behavioral and educational. New skills were taught gradually, progress was rewarded, and there was a lot of reinforcement.

My mother remembered that our teachers always made

eye contact with us, something autistic children find hard to do, but our teachers did it to us almost fiercely and we began to respond. They also always shook our hands when we arrived and when we left. Studies on this type of intensive behavioral intervention have shown twenty-point-plus gains in IQ over two to three years, as compared to control groups, and twenty-five per cent better results on language tests. All the studies have been relatively small-scale but such gains are close to overwhelming in a field where even small improvements have enormous human consequences. My parents regularly quoted one of these studies when they spoke about my school in New York, especially when they were explaining to other people that, even at the age of five, they did indeed let their son sometimes stay away in the school at weekends.

Ira stopped speaking and we were silent again. The outside of my glass was now clear of all condensation. Perhaps it was inevitable that it would work like this. After all, we didn't know one another. She knew me only as a child. I didn't know her at all. And yet everything I said to her, or so I presumed, would be panned for evidence that established the link or the trajectory between the child that she knew and the adult who sat before her now. I was afraid of that. I was afraid that I might not have come on enough. Did I beat the curve identified by the studies? Might she have expected me to do better than I had?

It was also becoming apparent to me that Ira had no intention of easing my discomfort. She had spotted it, for sure; perhaps she thought that I was grown-up enough to manage, that she was allowed to toy with me. I grinned as I realized that this might be the explanation.

'You're a mean person,' I said.

'You're not autistic,' she replied.

*

Rebecca exacted an entirely different silence from me when we met three days earlier, on the stairs outside our former school. I apologized for being late and, ignoring that, she motioned for me to sit down next to her.

'Do you remember sitting here?' she asked.

'Yes,' I replied after a pause, 'though I don't remember whether the view was the same as this, how the buildings that I can see from here have changed.'

She raised a finger and pressed it against my lips. 'Maybe sitting here is a test for your imagination and not your memory,' she suggested. I stopped talking but my imagination was inactive. I had thought a lot beforehand about meeting her and there were too many points highlighted in bold, spinning around in my head, for me to start imagining something new on her say-so. After a few minutes, I began tapping my toes gently, with a smile on my face, and she relented.

'Do you want to know what I saw?' she asked, standing up.

'Daisy chains and children playing on jungle gyms?' I offered.

She laughed and shook her head. Her grip on the line of the conversation relaxed. 'The news-stand where I used to buy the newspaper that I read to you guys has turned huge,' she exclaimed, standing up. 'We can go and look at it and then stop somewhere.'

The steps were the closest we were going to get to the school – it had closed around fifteen years earlier. My call to the building manager the night before meeting Rebecca was met with a weary, combative bafflement, as if the building manager's entire day had been structured around a stream of such nostalgic, otherworldly or impractical requests – he quickly said no. Rebecca and I noted, as we were leaving, that at least the new front door was attractive. I told her that, by chance, I had happened to visit New York shortly after the building was sold; it was in the midst of a refurbishment. I had got to look around but it was like any building site, gutted and generic, and the walk through didn't spur many thoughts. I only remember noticing that, with the rearrangement of its insides, it was somehow as if all the floors and windows had gone back to being at the levels that I would have viewed them at as a child.

It wasn't clear to me though why the school closed – my parents didn't know the story, only that they had been asked for money more often in the couple of years before it did shut down. Rebecca shrugged her shoulders when I raised it.

'Was it empty?' I asked, plaintively.

'What do you mean?' she murmured.

'Were there no students left? Did new schools open? Did the public school system improve its provision of care?'

'Ira called us into a room,' Rebecca explained. 'She wept to begin with. Then she called us to order and explained that the school was going to close because a major benefactor had pulled out. Then she pressed both her hands down hard on her desk and stood there until we all felt too embarrassed and started leaving.' As she paused, she grabbed her hair in both her hands and pulled it back, as if she was putting on a swimming cap. 'I think that was really all that happened.' She paused again, uncrossed and recrossed her arms. 'I think that I tried to broach the subject with her in the restroom one morning but she was sort of vague about it and said that no new money had been identified, that we'd rifled through what was left and that she'd run out of phone numbers to dial. Something like that. So we closed. I lost my job.'

When Ira hired her, Rebecca had no professional background in working with special needs children. The closure of the school was badly timed for her. Between the time when Ira first met her and she began looking for a new job, there had been a change in how special needs education was delivered. Ira was impressed by her careful manner and extrapolated from that, but Rebecca learnt that few other people were especially impressed either by that or by the experience she had gained in our school. Without a qualification, or the right accreditation, potential employers regarded those years as formative, vaguely beneficial, in the same way as university admissions officers might consider membership of an after-school maths club, experience in typesetting the graduation yearbook, or proficiency in playing the French horn. Those people who were interested in her experience, who asked her to tell them about it, none of them had a job to offer her. Over time, in interviews, or whenever she talked about these issues, she became more and more self-effacing. She explained that she was delighted that teaching for special needs children was more professionalized, that there were scores of learning workshops, supplementary texts – this was all wonderful, and no doubt it was a problem that she had very little exposure to any of this – but wasn't there some small way in which she could help out? When she first began to explore career routes following Ira's announcement about the closure of our school, she talked about course design and her own ideas for how to structure intensive one-to-one sessions between teacher and student. By the time she had spent eighteen months failing to get a job, she talked about her sensitivity, that she kept calm without anyone noticing that she was trying to keep calm, that she'd perhaps be a useful classroom assistant.

She was eventually hired on that basis by a public school in upstate New York. There were five children there who had been diagnosed with autism spectrum disorder and the school had found it difficult to procure anyone with firmer qualifications. After her third interview, the head teacher finally took her glasses off, laid them on the table, rubbed her temples and asked Rebecca if she needed any help in finding a place to live. The workload was relatively light. None of the parents agreed to leave their children in school after hours for additional one-to-one work, and the head teacher refused to accept Rebecca's argument that the five children needed a separate course of study if they were to prosper in the mainstream education system. So Rebecca nabbed every half-hour that she could with them and walked slowly past their classrooms from time to time, in case a teacher might spot her and decide to make use of her; she strove to be available, from half an hour before school began and until half an hour afterwards; she spoke to their parents at any social event, innocuously, as if she had just happened to spot them, or wanted a biscuit from the plate lying next to where they were standing, but really as part of a long-range project that she described to her friends under the rubric: 'Winning their trust.'

She pre-empted the question that I wanted to ask but for which I hadn't found a polite phrasing. We had moved on from our school to Central Park and were probably lost.

'I did good work back in that building,' she announced. We'd been silent for a couple of minutes and I was looking at her feet; her toes pointed forward throughout every stride.

'I'd spent eighteen months not doing what I was good at and now I was spending more time not doing it. And that's stupid. Not getting to do what you're good at is stupid.'

*

Three days later, as Rebecca joined Ira and me at the café, I remembered the look of annoyance on her face as she said those words. I realized that I wanted to explore this further, this question of motive. Rebecca and Ira greeted each other formally. Noticing this, I extended my hand, to one then the other. 'My name is Kamran,' I said. 'Apparently I'm not autistic.'

I should admit that I expected both Ira and Rebecca to have bad reasons for continuing to work with special needs children. Ira was in private practice but had been in private practice for long enough that she could afford to waive fees for families on lower incomes. Rebecca, by now, co-ordi- nated the special needs programs of a number of schools in her patch of New York State. I expected, unfairly, for there to be something martyr-like about them both. I expected that they viewed helping autistic children as a selfless and noble cause and that they wanted it to be acknowledged as such by other people. After all, there are few rewards to be derived from relationships with autistic children. Autistic children do not typically know that they are being helped out. They do not form a bond with the carer. They regularly resist even the embrace of their parents, so any additional carer is remoter still on their map of significance. And they don't necessarily get better. Rebecca's feeling, for example, was that she made no difference whatsoever to the five children at the school where she was first employed after her enforced career break of eighteen months.

I expected therefore that the reason why Rebecca and Ira worked with autistic children was to know that they did something difficult and unrewarding, and that it was this that made them feel better. This was a harsh view, I knew. But then I was also suspicious of people who talked about giving to charity. I sympathized with the tiny minority of Islamic scholars who argued that, in spite of the many references to the value of congregational prayer in scripture and in the teachings of the Prophet Muhammad, it should be avoided as it could easily become a pride-inducing public display of piety, soul-harming peacockery. And I had seen the way that Mike treated Randall; I had, unfortunately, got to the point of wondering whether Mike was with Randall because being with an autistic person, taking care of an autistic person, meant that Mike was morally well, that using his family's money to give Randall things and maintain him in an impressive house meant that it was OK to have that money.

I was glad to find that Rebecca and Ira's motives were different. Rebecca had only ever taken an eighteen-month, unwanted break from working with autistic children. Ira began working a day a week at another private school in New York shortly before our school closed down and moved there full-time, without any sort of a break, immediately afterwards. She was there for seven years before moving into solo practice in a room that, incidentally, was also lined with red carpet.

They both worked hard at their jobs but they also proselytized about what they did. It was important to take every opportunity to talk about the need for special education. It was important to impress on every parent that there was no shame in autism and that if their child did display any of the symptoms – insert list – they must talk to a specialist as soon as it could be arranged and stamp their feet if the local medical establishment was obstructive. They felt like religious evangelicals sometimes, as if they were bidding everyone to come to the way of the Lord on a Sunday and not to drink so much alcohol. But while people making those injunctions faced sneeriness and sarcasm when they spoke to colleagues and acquaintances, Rebecca and Ira faced something different. The reason why their interlocutors were reluctant to engage was not because they were clear and rational, confident that the funk and fervor of religion wasn't for them, but because they felt ashamed, that if their child did have developmental difficulties it was a private matter, and that they would fix it by overcoming their own failings as parents.

This view, of the parent as sinner, is even present in the scientific literature on autism. Leo Kanner was the first clinician to categorically diagnose autism, that is, to make the case for autism as a distinct developmental disorder, separate from, for example, retardation or juvenile schizophrenia. A bulk of analysis, including contributions from a series of other specialists, quickly formed around his claim.

Autism entered the diagnostic manuals used by psychiatrists and pediatricians. Having introduced this explanation, though, and given credence to the observations of many doctors and parents and initiated a process of further exploration, Kanner himself began lecturing, often aggressively, on the cause of autism, which he summarized in the term 'refrigerator mothers'.

As Ira was explaining this to me, at our table in the café, I realized that Rebecca was watching me rather than Ira. Was Ira doing the same when Rebecca spoke? Perhaps it was odd that, after twenty years, we were having this discussion first, about professionalism in special needs education, rather than a more personal one. But then I trusted them more for not having asked me a generic question such as, 'How are you?' or 'What have you been doing with yourself?' They were looking at me, though, and with Ira's provocation – undoing my diagnosis of autism – still hanging, it seemed that we would creep up on more intimate subjects in time.

I helped. As Ira took sip a of coffee, I noted that the term 'refrigerator mothers' made me think of the trick that my mother used to play on me as a child. Sometimes I'd watch a television commercial for chocolate or another sugary treat and I'd turn to her expectantly; she'd reach down a box that she kept high up in a kitchen cabinet and give me a sweet from it. It was only very much later that I learnt that the box was full of walnuts and almonds and, until then, I made no distinction between what I had seen advertised and the healthy snack that I received instead. Perhaps 'refrigerator mothers' were the opposite of this. Perhaps they yielded treats very easily to their children, behaved like refrigerators do, proud of their wares.

There was a pause until I prompted Ira by adding that Kanner, obviously, was evoking refrigerators in a different way. She nodded and resumed. His metaphor identified mothers who were cold towards their children, imposing, impassive, immoveable. Such mothers failed to provide their children with the affection that they needed to grab hold of in order to emerge into the social world. Hence they became emotionally handicapped, remained confined to their private realms.

Kanner's tag has buzzed around inside the heads of the parents of autistic children for a long time. Similar ideas are prevalent too. Another interpretation has it that autism occurs primarily among the children of upper-middle-class families. Though that incidence can be explained by the readier access to diagnosis for such families – private schooling with closer teacher attention, private healthcare, more friends who are medical professionals and thus spot things – some clinicians attribute the correlation between socio-economic status and autism to the attitudes of the parents. They argue that parents from upper-middle-class families frequently have very high expectations of their children; a child may not meet those expectations, or may meet them and then be confronted with yet more elevated ones. One way or another, eventually the child feels that it is failing and so begins to withdraw. That withdrawal increases the parents' anxiety, or leads them to withdraw too – the net result is that the child is left untethered and starts to fall into autism.

The salience of these notions made it difficult for Ira and Rebecca to engage parents and put proper care plans in place for their children. Ira set down her coffee cup and described a sample situation. A child was admitted to our school shortly after being diagnosed. The child was four years old and his language skills were rudimentary. He regularly ran into things, at knee height, tummy height, even head height, and seemed not to care. His body was spotted with purple and blue bruises. There was briefly a question mark about physical abuse at home but it was ruled out soon after he joined the school and his recklessness in throwing his body around was observed by others. He had a relatively successful first three months and then suddenly stopped attending. Ira sent letters and placed phone calls but made no progress, and so decided to visit the house.

It was a Saturday afternoon. She knew that she would be denied an appointment and so she pretended that she was in the area visiting a friend. She walked down the street from the opposite end, picking an address and adding a name to constitute her alibi. The parents let her in. They were amiable to begin with. She stood in the kitchen admiring the vast quantity of flowers that they were arranging into vases. But the tone changed when she asked them about their son. She didn't even say very much. As she remembered it, she had only asked where he was now going to school, did it have provision for developmental therapy and, if not, might they agree to one-to-one sessions? At that point, the mother pressed both of her palms hard against the table in the middle of the room, as if she was about to perform a handstand on it, and began shouting, and the father threw a vase. The vase struck Ira on her right arm, which she had raised to protect her chest, and shattered. When she got her breath back, Ira discovered that she was cut, that she was bleeding profusely. She lowered herself to the floor as she was afraid that she would faint. 'Call me an ambulance,' she yelled and the father came over to take a look. He knelt down beside her and, in a quiet voice, made her promise that she would lie about how her injury had occurred before he signaled to his wife to dial 911.

'That was a courageous thing to do, to go over there like that,' I suggested, blinking, a little short of breath on hearing Ira's shocking story.

'I would do the same if I were a cancer specialist and a patient of mine discontinued treatment,' Ira shrugged. 'I'd want to make sure we had a proper conversation before I put the file in the trash.'

'Plus these are children we're talking about,' added Rebecca. She examined Ira's face for a moment before speaking. Rebecca deferred to Ira, I noticed, perhaps in the way that nurses defer to doctors, or simply the way that people defer to senior colleagues. After all, Ira had once been her employer.

Ira nodded. 'The child was my student, is what it comes down to. Not only did I need to know that the decision had been made in an informed way, I also needed to know that the decision had been made with the child's best interests at the core. Clearly the child didn't make the decision himself. He wasn't able to. No child that age is. Which makes what we do especially difficult.'

I was nodding as she spoke. I was enjoying this. Obviously I didn't like to think of Ira lying on the floor, bleeding, being coerced into ceding her professional conscience, but I was realizing that she didn't go to that house to win the gratitude of the parents – she wasn't there to press a sponge to the child's head and heal its pain – she was there for her patient, because she was rigorous about her duty of care. It was important, I felt, that we, in our school, had been with professionals, not blithe spirits.

The economy of care has changed and the new paradigm of professionally administered care that Rebecca and Ira are part of appeals to me more than that of nuns and nun-like women. I didn't want to be sitting at that café table feeling indebted to Rebecca and Ira, and I don't think that they wanted me to be feeling that way either. They didn't fix me and I didn't give their lives a glowing, uncomplicated purpose – this wasn't the quid pro quo that was agreed between us.

Of course, something was also being lost in the historical change; there was cause for nostalgia. The new paradigm set carers and those cared for further apart. The bond between Rebecca, Ira and me was a formal one. I was not the son they never had, or the son they sent to war, having brought up, and didn't see again until now. I was a student for whose care they had been paid by an institution, for whose care they had followed certain standards and guidelines, for whose care their responsibility ended at a determinate point. They weren't clutching my hands, as we sat together now, twenty years later, and pulling out photographs of me as a child. I wasn't buying them perfume or leather-bound notebooks. Perhaps this formality lessened their satisfaction. Or perhaps it made it easier to assess me critically, to observe unflinchingly the effect of certain techniques, and that improved treatment made it more likely that their care would help me and others like me.

But if this paradigm was right, if it led to better results, that also meant that all the schools who declined to hire Rebecca after she left ours were right to do so. Professional expertise was more critical than eloquently expressed concern, which was all that Rebecca had.

'Plus experience,' Ira corrected, as I blurted out this thought and before Rebecca had a chance to respond herself. 'Skills aren't usually learnt in universities.'

'Ah,' I said, realizing my error. I'd just offended Rebecca; I was suddenly sure of it. I focussed on correcting my posture for a moment.

'But you did mean *extremely* eloquently expressed concern?' she teased, breaking her silence. She placed her hand on mine for a moment and I nodded.

The waitress had handed us a long list of cheesecakes around twenty minutes earlier, but each time that she had hovered nearby to take our order we were talking. She took her opportunity now and approached our table, bringing fresh glasses of water. Both Rebecca and Ira were successful in placing their orders, but my first choice was unavailable, as was my second. As the waitress asked me to try again, I was aware of being watched closely by both Rebecca and Ira, at this moment of fracture, as if there was a danger that I might not know what to do next. Or perhaps I was being over-sensitive, squirming too hard and imagining too much intent into their medicalized gaze.

My third attempt to place an order was successful and, as the waitress left, I reached down into my bag and pulled out a notebook.

'Who would you like to hear about first?' I asked. I had practiced for this. Though I had told my classmates a little about each other, this was going to be my first go at running through the entire narrative of meeting them again and spending time with them. I was going to try it with the names and other details already changed, so that I could begin to get used to the discipline by which I had promised to protect their private lives. Rebecca and Ira would be able to work out who was who but they'd also be able to guide me on whether the changes were sufficient to divert other people.

Rebecca spoke first. 'We've discussed this,' she began, looking over at Ira then engaging me. 'We'd rather read about them in your book.'

I placed both my hands on the table to prevent them fidgeting by my sides. 'I don't understand.' This was supposed to be the centerpiece of our meeting.

'We thought that you might take this in a variety of different ways,' Rebecca continued. 'At worst, you'd assume that we didn't trust your judgment in describing your former classmates – but that can't be right as why would we then want to read your book? So we hoped that you would quickly get to the best version. You'd reason that we didn't want to alter your observations. Yours are the ones that matter here.' As Rebecca finished talking, she gestured towards Ira.

'You're the one who met them,' Ira added.

'But you're autistic?' remarked Rebecca. They were feeding each other lines. They had prepared for my reaction.

'Oh, don't worry about that,' assured Ira. 'He isn't anymore.'

I closed over my notebook as the waitress came back with our cheesecakes. What Rebecca and Ira had just said to me was incredibly generous, I realized, as well as flattering. I also grasped that they wanted, apparently more than I did, a conversation between three adults. It was me who was still seeing them as teachers and myself as their tiny student. I wanted to return to that dynamic; they didn't. I found myself thinking of the night that Ira had peeled my face from the window on the second floor of our school. It must have been one of the weekends when some of us stayed over. I wasn't able to sleep. I got out of bed and sat down in the window-seat where I could look down on to the street or into the trees. I must have fallen asleep sitting there like that, and my cheek came to rest against the window-pane. It was a cold night and, when I woke, my cheek was stuck to the glass. In that position, I couldn't yell properly, or even cry properly. But Ira was either passing by or heard one of my constricted yelps and she came and tore me off the window-pane. She may not remember this, though. And why would I raise it?

'Now there's a different sense of shame about autism,' remarked Rebecca, after we had each gobbled half of our desserts. Taking us back to an earlier discussion, she began to speak of a father who moped around her classroom door at least once a week. Even though he drove a fair way to get to the school and had to leave work early to do so, she always had to invite him in and initiate the conversation. He asked about his son's progress. He asked whether there were foods that he should be cutting out of his son's diet, nutrients that he should be supplementing it with; could he borrow some more flashcards so that he could do some work with his son in the evenings?

As Rebecca explained, the prevalent view is no longer that nurture or, as Kanner would have it, that the lack of nurture, causes autism but that autism is natural, that it is genetically determined. There isn't quite enough evidence, as the pool for any research is relatively small, and as research in this direction hasn't been going for long. Nevertheless, studies suggest that the risk for siblings of autistic individuals is higher than the risk for anyone else. The concordance rate for monozygotic twins, that is, twins who share all of their genetic material, is estimated at around sixty per cent. The rate for dizygotic twins, that is, twins who share half of their genetic material, is around the same as for other siblings.

These findings pull in the same direction. While the sibling recurrence rate can be explained by nurture – i.e. put crudely, a mother who refrigerated her first child may refrigerate a subsequent child too – the rate for monozygotic twins is so much higher than both the rate for dizygotic twins and other siblings that it suggests genes do play a significant role. There are more family studies being done, which are expected to validate these results, and there is, in any case, a much broader trend towards genetic explanations in all genres of medicine. Parents might not therefore *cause* autism in their children, but they probably do pass it on.

It gets worse. The loci for autism on the genome have not been pinpointed, but some analysis suggests that between three and ten genes are involved in autism, and other interpretations have it that as many as one hundred genes might be involved. If the higher estimates are accurate, this means that many more people have some, or even a plurality, of the genes for autism than display the symptoms for it. Autism is caused by rare mutations among these – up to one hundred – genes. This, in the middle of a sleepless night, to a parent whose child has just been diagnosed, means not only that you have passed on the potential for autism to your baby through your genes but also that the child has developed autism, by virtue of one or more or countless mutations, while you have not.

This is genuinely difficult. In the case of any condition with some element of genetic causation, no parent is glad when their child is born with the same condition that they have, but they realize that, over time, they will share challenges, they will be able to examine in common what they have in common. However, in a sort of variation of survivor's guilt, if your child is autistic and you are not, to know that autism is genetic – that it is, technically speaking, something you both have in common – simply extends the distance between the two of you; it has the potential to introduce many more prickles into your interaction, to impair your understanding of one another rather than ease it.

Ira believed that parents' propensity to believe that autism was caused by vaccines or by mercury poisoning – both popular explanations much touted on the Internet – was due to this lingering, perhaps renewed, sense of shame about having a child with a developmental disorder. It was simpler for everyone if autism had a material cause and, ideally, one external to the relationship between parent and child. It wasn't ridiculous for parents, for example, to believe that a particular vaccine may trigger autism. The symptoms of autism were often not noticed until a child was due to begin speaking or started spending more time with other children. Vaccines were administered at around the same age. The two events might easily be connected by parents who naturally preferred an explanation for their child's autism that didn't involve their own DNA, or who wanted to set aside the quizzical looks from their friends wondering if maybe they were bad parents.

Ira explained that she saw the MMR vaccine story as continuous with older stories about changelings. There was a powerful folk tradition, in many parts of the world, about children who were abducted and replaced by fairies, or other creatures disguised as children. Ira gave us an example that Martin Luther told. I've looked it up since and it's worth quoting formally.

Eight years ago at Dessau, I, Dr. Martin Luther, saw and touched a changeling. It was twelve years old, and from its eyes and the fact that it had all of its senses, one could have thought that it was a real child. It did nothing but eat; in fact, it ate enough for any four peasants or threshers. It ate, defecated, and urinated, and whenever someone touched it, it cried. When bad things happened in the house, it laughed and was happy; but when things went well, it cried. It had these two virtues. I said to the Princes of Anhalt: 'If I were the prince or the ruler here, I would throw this child into the water – into the Molda that flows by Dessau. I would dare commit murder!' But the Elector of Saxony, who was with me at Dessau, and the Princes of Anhalt did not want to follow my advice. Therefore, I said: 'Then you should have all Christians repeat the Lord's Prayer in church that God may exorcise the devil.' They did this daily at Dessau, and the changeling child died in the following year . . . Such a changeling child is only a piece of flesh, a *massa carnis*, because it has no soul.

Arguably, this child is displaying the symptoms of autism. Autistic children often react badly to being touched. They

201

find it overwhelming and they may cry to ward it off. It was unlikely that the child always laughed when bad things happened in the house and cried when the atmosphere was jollier; however, it would not be surprising for an autistic child to have failed to notice how others in the house felt and to have sustained its own version of events.

Martin Luther's remedy of exorcism, though it had tragic effects, was gentler than other remedies that might be derived from similar tales about changelings. There were stories that culminated in burning or drowning or other forms of disguised infanticide. In one example from the West Country in England, a farmer's youngest son was stolen and replaced by a sickly, sallow, silent imp of a boy. The farmer and his wife raised the queer new child as their own. However, some years later, a pixie appeared at their door. 'Father!' the boy cried out. The pair ran off and, in true fairy-tale form, the farm was blessed with good fortune from that day forwards. The child did not always disappear or die though. Often the act, or even the threat, of violence caused the changeling to vanish and the parents' real child to return.

Ira also believed that stories about feral children were stories about children with developmental disorders. However, these were not children who grew up in the wild and thereby had developmental problems; these were children who were left in the wild because of their difficulties. Parents despaired, led them into the woods, departed, and the accounts that we have of feral children are accounts of those children who survived long enough to be found; many more of these so-called feral children will have perished, she conjectured, stabbing at the air with her fingertips, usually within days of being abandoned.

Rebecca went quiet during this part of the conversation and concentrated on finishing her cheesecake. Yet she had originally introduced the theme. When I had seen Rebecca three days earlier, she spoke about a mother she had met recently. Rebecca didn't teach her child; she hadn't met the child. However, she had been introduced to the mother at a friend's house and the mother learnt that Rebecca worked with autistic children and revealed that her own son was autistic. The mother then explained, in a flat, unwavering tone, that her son contracted autism when, one evening, she took him out to their roof terrace after dinner. She spotted a shooting star and she pointed it out to him. He watched it closely but then it suddenly disappeared from his view. She could still see it but, despite all of her pointing, he couldn't find it again. Subsequent to that evening, he became quieter, more difficult to handle; he smashed the door of the washing machine at the onset of one of his tantrums. She took him to a doctor and the diagnosis was one of autism. From watching her behavior, it was obvious to Rebecca that the mother fell within the autism spectrum herself. She hugged herself very tight when she spoke, as if you might want to take her hands and make her say something that she didn't want to say. Her voice was flat. Rebecca told her about the language devel-opment problems faced by many autistic children and learnt that the mother had been slow to start speaking herself. She was eight before her parents had sent her to school. Later, after she had gone, Rebecca's friend apologized, explained that the boy's mother was receiving medication for border-line schizophrenia, that the autistic child was now living with the father.

Rebecca remarked, on passing me the story, that the

mother was sincere in her account of how her child developed autism but that the story was also an admission of inadequacy and inarticulacy. It made the tiny hairs on her forearms stand on end; to hear the mother talk about the shooting star was to experience a woman who felt guilty and was unable to mitigate that guilt. As Ira spoke about changeling myths and feral children, it seemed to me that Rebecca must have been thinking of this mother. This mother, still in shock about her child becoming unwell, could only for the moment tell a story about a fateful shooting star, like the parents who denied that the child was even theirs, who needed to say that it belonged to the fairies instead, that their own child had been taken. It was terribly sad, these parents, throbbing with guilt and shame, using whatever resources they could find in the culture, whatever external cause they could identify, to exculpate themselves.

And yet Rebecca didn't speak during Ira's exposition. I suddenly worried that I had set up a meeting not with two of my old teachers, during which we could talk together about all things, but with Rebecca and her old boss. I worried that Rebecca and I had established a sort of parity between ourselves when we met three days earlier, but that Rebecca felt subordinate to Ira and that, by letting Ira speak in grand sweeps, admiring her scope, I was contributing to that feeling.

Rebecca had also told me, when we met previously, about the time Ira spent in autism activism. I considered this as Ira paused. Ira was dismissive of the MMR vaccine and the mercury poisoning accounts of how autism began but she was zealous about gluten, Rebecca had revealed, especially during her years as an activist.

There is evidence to suggest that a large proportion of autistic children experience difficulties with gluten intolerance, food allergies or malabsorption of nutrients. This prompts the thought that autistic children are unable to derive the right nutrients from their diet and that, through suffering inflammation, their digestive systems also become prone to attack by microbes such as *Candida albicans* – which experts hold responsible for certain immune disorders and ME. On this thesis, autism is caused due to the failure of the digestive system to extract the right nutrients for the child's brain and the concurrent inefficacy in warding off dangerous microbes. This has demonstrable material effects – for example, autistic children can have very low levels of serotonin, which are frequently associated with clinical depression – and, potentially, a deeper impact on development which we are not yet able to fully explain.

By removing gluten from the diet, this argument continues, it is possible to restore proper functioning of the digestive system and thereby promote good absorption of nutrients. Inflammation decreases and the immune system begins to return to normal. Once the immune system is returned to adequate levels, it also begins to keep the microbes in the intestines in proper balance. Ira had become an advocate of a therapeutic diet regimen based on this thesis. In the beginning, it allowed simple carbohydrates but prohibited complex ones; the child's digestive system needed training. After the introductory diet, the next stage of the diet allowed many more foods, but required that all fruits and vegetables be peeled, deseeded, and cooked in order to make them more easily digestible. By removing the foods that could not be properly broken down, the energy source for the unwanted microbes was eliminated. The vicious cycle of malabsorption, inflammation, and food allergies seen in children with autism was broken and healthy digestion began.

It seemed a difficult concept to agitate for. It didn't involve petitions to state legislatures or impassioned radio interviews but long shopping trips, careful browsing in supermarkets, dedicated recipe books, and consultation sessions in health-food stores. However, I could see why it appealed to parents. It gave them a role. As Rebecca had described, the father who brooded outside her classroom liked to borrow flashcards so that he could do the right sort of activities with his child at home.

Though it is important for professionals to take the lead in designing care plans for children with developmental conditions, informed by clinical experience and the latest literature, most parents want to play a part too. There are a very few parents who, upon diagnosis, climb down a well, begin believing that their child will always be this way, and submit to extra lessons and buy helpful computer programs only due to peer pressure, rather than out of hope. A sizeable majority of parents though read a lot of books, visit websites, email one another through networks, attend conferences, hurry around looking for anything that glitters. Especially if food allergies or maldigestion are the causes of autism, parents can, and need to, get involved in a very detailed way; the palliative care is process-led and simple; every shopping trip and every meal becomes an opportunity to assist.

It isn't just wishful thinking, either. There is an evidential base for it. Studies clearly show that many autistic children do have food allergies and serious digestive problems – though my subsequent email to my former classmates, following these discussions with Rebecca and Ira, yielded only a mild lactose intolerance and an allergy to bee stings (both from Randall). There are well-established links between digestion and overall health. And there is emerging evidence that antidepressants, especially Selective Serotonin Re-uptake Inhibitors (SSRIs), tend to reduce the severity of autistic symptoms in some individuals. If increasing the presence of serotonin in the brain through pharmaceuticals can help with autism, then eliminating digestive problems that depress the production of serotonin may help for the same, albeit still somewhat obscure, reasons.

The central problem is the same as with behavioral interventions such as the aggressive eye contact that Ira practiced on us as children, or the computer program that she described earlier when we first sat down. These techniques work but their success doesn't tell us enough about the condition itself. It is likely that serotonergic function has some role in autism but it is unlikely that a single neurotransmitter can adequately explain the entire phenomenon of autism. An analogy might be that the existence of water, though key to life, doesn't quite explain why we are here. More work is needed on broader trends in the autistic brain. And while this is underway, dedicated research into autism is a recent development and funds remain limited. Presumably the single greatest boon for autism research is likely to be the interest of the big pharmaceutical companies; however, just as deseeding fruits and vegetables isn't going to turn autistic children into the cynosures of their playgroup, a single drug isn't likely to close down all special needs schools and banish

Tom and Maureen into oblivion – and that reduces the financial incentive for these companies.

'Did you ever join an advocacy organization?' I asked Ira, turning to Rebecca, who blinked very hard at me, as if I had just explained that the next big advance in superstring theory could be derived from a cave painting in Cornwall.

'Who told you about that?' replied Ira gently, after a pause, as if each word was a pebble and she was running her fingers over them individually. From her tone of voice, I realized that I had screwed up. I had wanted to bring Rebecca back into the conversation by challenging Ira, by bringing up this embarrassing portion of her past, but it was only after I spoke that I realized that Rebecca and Ira knew each other much better than they knew me, and so it wasn't really my task to mediate between them. Rebecca turned her head to one side and grinned. None of the waiting staff were close by. In any case, neither my coffee cup nor my water glass were empty. I discovered that I had already placed my right hand in my pocket and that I was looking for a crocodile clip that was not there.

'I understand,' I began to say eventually, 'that . . .'

'It's OK,' Ira motioned. 'It's OK.' She tapped on the table. 'I was part of an advocacy organization. Then I decided to come back to private practice. Why did I do that?' She scrunched up her face and then released it again. 'I prefer intensive work. I think that it's just that. I prefer intensive work, work that I can do with autistic individuals directly.'

This was often a dilemma, I understood, from her expression. There was a felicific calculus to be worked through between work that was direct and personal, on one side, and work that was global and systemic on the other. I knew civil servants who preferred to work in social security offices and others for whom abstract policy analysis was more suitable. These were professional choices – sometimes they were guided by consideration of what would be better in career terms over a long span, but they were also sentimental and expressive choices; sometimes they were about what was the most good that I can do now, what I can do to be worthwhile. I felt embarrassed for asking Ira about this. I felt embarrassed that I had come at it this way. Quite aside from the fact that I was trying to rebalance a conversation between two friends, and this wasn't really my prerogative, surely I didn't know Rebecca and Ira well enough to ask them questions that seemed to require that they enter into explanation and self-justification. Why have you spent your life the way that you have? Set out for me the grounds for the complex choices that you have made. This was what I kept asking them.

'Have you ever joined an advocacy organization?' asked Rebecca. Out of the corner of my eye, it looked like she was examining my cheek.

'I haven't,' I replied.

Craig told me about a meeting that he attended once. It was the monthly get-together of an organization founded, essentially, on the basis that people like Rebecca and Ira were trying to eradicate a distinctive way of being and that there was a need to stop them. According to this heterodoxy, autism was not a developmental disorder. People who were autistic suffered no lack, their symptoms were not shortcomings; these were simply the characteristics of the autistic individual and the way of life and the style of thought of the autistic individual was as valid as what clinicians defined as 'normal'.

The members of organizations like that one were not the first to hold these views. A number of intellectuals, including the philosopher Jean-Jacques Rousseau, had drawn similar conclusions from observing feral children. The 'Wild Boy of Aveyron', named Victor after he was found, was one of the most famous – though according to Ira, purported – examples of a feral child. He was discovered in the late eighteenth century in the forests of Aveyron, France, and became a fixture in the royal court. There are accounts of state occasions where he bounded around the room, shed his clothes, climbed trees, and gulped berries from shrubs in the grounds. He had no manners and no conception of them. A guest at one of these occasions observed:

> [He] hardly heeded the beautiful eyes whose attention he himself attracted. When dessert was served, and he had adroitly filled his pockets with all the delicacies that he could filch, he calmly left the table . . . Suddenly a noise came from the garden . . . We soon glimpsed [him] running across the lawn with the speed of a rabbit . . . he had stripped to his undershirt. Reaching the main avenue of the park . . . he tore his last garment in two, as if it were simply made of gauze; then, climbing the nearest tree with the ease of a squirrel, he perched in the middle of the branches.

Obviously there were those who were outraged by his antics, but there were also those who were drawn to him, who understood his abandon as true authenticity, who admired his freedom from social mores, distinctions of class, and the conventions of their company.

There is a set of contemporary movements that draws on similar themes. There are groups of people diagnosed with schizophrenia who contend that their condition became something negative only due to the way it was classified by the medical profession and by society more broadly. It is others who made it into an illness, whereas, for themselves, it is simply a way of being, with good points and bad points. Similarly, there are associations of deaf people who believe that sign language has the same status as the languages of Amerindian tribes or Micronesian island communities and that advanced hearing aids and the drive of doctors to install them represent an attempt to eradicate what is distinctive about the lives of deaf people.

Craig didn't stay at the meeting that he attended. The premise was that you could be extraordinary and distinctive purely on account of being autistic, that this was a creative and valuable way of being, equal to being a poet or a woodsman. Craig didn't accept that. He felt that it was exactly the same as believing that all autistic individuals were retarded or that all autistic children were savants and could multiply six-digit numbers instantaneously. Being autistic didn't conclude any issues of identity or any questions of how you live your life or what makes it valuable. I agreed with Craig and set this out to Rebecca and Ira.

'But there must be things that you do better than other people?' asked Ira, turning her palms up towards the sky. 'And you must think that being autistic contributes to some of them?'

'I haven't thought about it very much,' I replied.

None of my former classmates provided obvious examples. Randall was a good bicycle courier, he understood the city very well, but so did the other riders, and it was unlikely that his ability existed due to autism; considering that Elizabeth couldn't manage maps, and had to count bus stops instead, Randall's ability existed, it seemed, *despite* autism. Elizabeth was an able musician, she could play back pieces of music after brief exposure, but no one ever counted on her ability to become a pianist. The only examples that I could recover were from my own experience, and they were considerably smaller in scope than perhaps Ira hoped.

I told them about being on the radio. I had done it once, briefly. I was seated in a narrow studio, in a different city from the presenter. It was the first time that I had done this sort of thing and I had not had a chance to think about what I might say. Without knowing what the questions were going to be, I was suddenly confronted with a microphone and a voice in my ears. I was then offered a cup of coffee, which I considered, because I could use it. I could take a sip between answers, it would provide focus, a little bit of coherence. And it would mean, in my own mind, that I was just drinking a cup of coffee and talking. Ultimately, however, I decided that the sound of sipping might be picked up by the microphone and that would not necessarily be pleasant for the listener.

I then noticed that there was a telephone in the studio. And so I put my hand on the telephone and closed my eyes when my turn came. Apparently I sounded fine. I was relaxed. I did OK. But it was because I convinced myself that I was talking on the telephone and that I was not doing something new or alien, or which had a much wider audience. Friends asked me afterwards if I was nervous, because I didn't seem to be. I replied vaguely, in case I might sound boastful, but I explained to Rebecca and Ira that I truly wasn't nervous; once I incorporated the telephone, I wasn't nervous at all. I wondered whether, perhaps, if I did not know to look for such strategies, if historically I had not needed to do this throughout my life, then perhaps I would have done less well in my radio performance.

I also thought of the photograph from my parents' trove in which I was on my knees; my father was sitting in front of me. It was a Saturday, he recalled, and he was happy to have his first Saturday at home at the end of a bad stretch of working weekends. My mother was out visiting friends. My father was playing with me. There was a big piece of paper in front of me. I had a large purple crayon in my right hand. And that was odd.

I was left-handed, I explained to Rebecca and Ira. I had always been left-handed. Some older people in my family weren't happy about it. I remembered dinner in the house of a distant relative. An old man sitting next to me rapped my knuckles whenever I tried to pick up a piece of food with my left hand. Sometimes still, in South Asian or Arabic restaurants, someone discreetly reminds me that the devil does his best work with his left hand. I could not use my right hand however. I especially could not use it to draw or to write. If I tried, it looked like I was reproducing an ancient language. If I tried, after a while, my hand felt like it was filling up slowly with water and then emptying again.

Nevertheless, there was a photograph in which I was holding a crayon in my right hand and the crayon was pressed against the paper. From time to time, I thought of this photograph and I tried to work out why I might have been using my right hand. I wondered if my left hand was injured. But my parents didn't recall an injury. I wondered if I was testing my right hand. Perhaps I didn't have a concept of handedness at that time. Perhaps I had seen other children use their right hand and I wanted to do so too. But I am not holding the crayon very well. The grip is different than other photographs in which I am drawing with my left hand. By the time of the photograph, I was plainly aware that I could not draw with my right hand. Yet I was trying to.

I did not work out the reason until I read *The Silent Child* by Laurent Danon-Boileau, Professor of General Linguistics at the University of Paris. He described six children who did not speak, or who spoke only a little. The second child was named Kim. Her father was Cambodian and her mother was Chinese. The family lived in France. The parents tried speaking to her in Cambodian, Chinese, and French. She did speak from time to time, but not in any of these languages.

Kim's language skills improved gradually over time. She learnt to take turns. She started using words from languages known to others. However, Danon-Boileau noted that she nevertheless took care to assign no more than one meaning to each word. Of course, most people are typically far less zealous in their use of words. They do not mind if some warp and weft enters into the lexicon, if words loosen themselves from what they signify – most jokes and the best sentences rely on some of this. However, for Kim, language was still tenuous, and she insisted that each word have only one referent. Every new meaning required a new word. Professor Danon-Boileau elaborated:

Th[e] quest for monovalence could be seen in her manner of drawing. Like all children, she sometimes wanted to cancel a sketch she had just made by crossing it out. But to do this, Kim would take her pencil in her other hand, as if her changed view of her drawing obliged her to break her ties with herself, as if the negative opinion were someone else's and she were thus the arena for two juxtaposed impulses: the wish to make the drawing, expressed by one hand, and the wish to cancel it, expressed by the other in the form of the crossed lines. There is no doubt that she was not doing this deliberately. It was a purely mechanical action. But it showed the difficulty Kim had in expressing two opposed points of view. She could not link together her wish to make a drawing and her rejection of that drawing. Hence the curious division of the two actions between her two hands.

When I read this passage, I recounted to Rebecca and Ira, I immediately thought of the photograph. I was there on my knees and the crayon was in my wrong hand. So this was what it was. A curious division of two actions between two hands. My father photographed me trying to cancel out a drawing that I had just made. I could not work out how I could have drawn it and I could not want to have drawn it. So the crayon went into the other hand. I knew that I could not hold a crayon properly in my right hand, but my action was mechanical. I needed to draw a line through my drawing and this impulse contradicted the previous one to make the drawing and I could not encompass both impulses easily. The crayon switched to my other hand and this eased my situation. My father clicked the shutter, capturing quite by chance one of my first attempts at local coherence.

I often thought about that photograph, and perhaps the

key point was to think about what another child would have done. It was possible that another child would have got upset and cried. Or become frustrated and spoilt the entire piece of paper, then stopped drawing. I wondered if it was only because I was autistic, and therefore alert to local coherence, that I thought of swapping hands and solving the problem in a remarkably rational, and seemingly calm, way.

Both my examples were trivial – overcoming anxiety about talking on the radio, drawing with a crayon at the age of three – but they did suggest that there were times when being autistic was an advantage. However, it was difficult to construct a political movement around moments such as these. These were not emblems of a valuable and distinctive way of life, in the way that spirituals or head-dresses may be for black culture, or meditation and haiku may be for the samurai. My achievements, if they can be called that, were worth remembering, but they were trivial, especially when set alongside the difficulties that autistic individuals faced and the hard, material symptoms such as delayed language development, an impaired sense of empathy, and the need for local coherence, satisfied simply through rocking or in subtler ways.

What I found myself arguing to Rebecca and Ira, with growing animation, was that it was arrogant to believe that I was better due to being autistic. Perhaps it did equip me well for certain things, perhaps some of these were not trivial, perhaps, for example, something of my intelligence was related to being autistic; however, I had only reached the threshold beyond which I could even have this discussion with them due, surely, to professional help, *their* professional help, and a lot of consideration, and work, and care.

'You almost want to feel disempowered,' remarked Rebecca with puzzlement. I paused. Had I really ended up arguing for this? Why? Was I trying to be the patient that they had cured and should feel good about? Was there nothing of me in it? I shook my head. I did feel strongly about this. I was surprised.

'Not at all,' I replied. 'I am able to be here and I am able to participate in this conversation and I am able to talk to both of you as I am doing, even though you were once my teachers, even though that should be paralyzingly frightening to me.'

Ira nodded. She looked directly into my eyes.

'To the contrary,' I continued, turning back to Rebecca, 'I feel empowered but there's no cause to disregard the reasons for my empowerment.'

Ira brought her hands together and pretended that she was about to clap. I felt thrilled. I felt as if I had broken something.

'Do you think that I'm autistic any more?' I asked Rebecca. The question tumbled out. I didn't mean to ask it. 'She doesn't,' I nodded my head towards Ira.

'She does not,' confirmed Ira.

Rebecca smiled and took my hand. 'I agree,' she replied. 'I was thinking about it just a moment ago. You ran this conversation from start to finish. More or less. So, yes, I agree. Is it important?'

I shook my head. It couldn't be important. Or I couldn't admit to them that it was important, but perhaps I'd think about it again later.

*

Eventually I told them about Elizabeth. I didn't want to. It had the potential to change the shading of our conversations.

217

It might be like brushing my hand roughly across Ira's red carpet. I understood that they didn't want to know the stories of the Idiots until they read about them here. But not to tell them about the fact of Elizabeth's suicide and to justify that under the terms of their injunction felt like sophistry.

Henry and Sheila didn't tell them. They told some of the other parents, the ones that they knew well. Henry wrote an email, at around 4 a.m., about eighteen hours after Elizabeth died. He wrote it while angry; it asked all the parents not to overextend their children, to keep them at home if possible, and not to allow them to have friends or lovers and certainly not to procreate.

I let Rebecca and Ira know about Elizabeth via email, too. It was a few weeks after we had met over coffee and cheesecake. Ira rang me immediately. I was still at my laptop, drawing circles on the track pad with my finger. I suppose that I was waiting for my head to clear. Ira didn't say hello.

'Why didn't they tell me?' she demanded. She was angry. 'Do you have any insight into why they didn't tell me?'

'I'm sorry that I didn't tell you before,' I replied. It was what I was thinking about when I hugged them goodbye after our conversation at the café. When I peered over their shoulders as they squeezed me in turn, I kept my eyes open; things seemed skewed to me, made odd junctions with one another, and I knew that I'd made an error and, already, that I'd need to unravel it later.

'Did they say anything about why they didn't tell me?' It was the voice, I imagined, that she might use with parents who had stopped sending their child to sessions. She'd ask open questions, I thought. She'd want to know *why* they weren't sending their child to sessions any more, not just try to convince them to change their mind.

'I didn't ask, Ira, I couldn't think of a way to ask them.'

She thought about this for a moment. I could feel her holding the phone away from her mouth as she did so. 'No, that's fair enough,' she remarked after the pause. 'But no reasons were volunteered?'

'We didn't talk about it. I didn't challenge them.'

Ira sighed. She signed off shortly thereafter.

Rebecca rang me too. She checked her email less frequently, so it wasn't until a couple of days later. The conversation went differently. She asked for more information. She asked about the piano lessons that Elizabeth taught. She asked about whether Elizabeth, when grown up, looked like her mother or her father. We both burst into tears briefly.

The last that I saw of Rebecca and Ira was as they re-engaged with New York following our long session at the café. I stayed at the table to start making notes, and watched them for some time after we said goodbye to one another. They left in different directions. I tried to follow their progress for as long as I could. I looked one way, then the other, back and forth. It was like cooking a meal that has two parts. Ira checked her watch, stood, thought for a moment, and then stepped out to the kerb to hail a taxi. She didn't look around her. A man bumped into her and she was very apologetic. Then she got in her taxi and went around a corner. Rebecca crossed the street. She stopped and read a notice in the window of a store that sold theater tickets. Next she paused by a news-stand. She knew that I was watching her. She bought a newspaper and waved it in the air. 'Send in the Idiots,' I mouthed and waved back, laughing.

Epilogue

THE FIRST PERSON TO interview André for college admission wore a scarf that was the same color as his shorts. The interview took place in his study. The chairs sighed as they sat down, as if they were weighing the occupants and noting the findings. The windows were divided into small sections and the room was covered in parallelograms of light, one of which stretched across his right leg; it looked like he was patch-testing a new hair color, or that this part of his leg was being softly smoked.

The interview was slow. The man in the shorts and the scarf held a clipboard and mechanically made his way through a list of questions. He told André, before the interview began, that he was entitled to think about any of the questions before replying and to ask for clarification if any of them were unclear. André paused an average of forty-five seconds before giving his answers. After each of the first three questions in the series, the interviewer unfolded his legs, leant forward, and told André that there was no reason to be nervous and that any question could be re-asked or rephrased for his convenience. André shook his head each time and answered when he was ready. About twenty-five minutes into the interview, the interviewer removed his scarf and placed it in his lap. About ten minutes after that, he asked André whether he had been able to continue his studies during the time that he spent in an institution for young offenders.

André paused for a little longer than his average before answering, and then explained that there was a special needs liaison officer who came to the institution once a week to see him because he was autistic. The interviewer unfolded his legs and leant forwards again. He asked André at what age he was diagnosed; he asked whether he had a photographic memory, and if he ever fell asleep listening to static on a bedside radio. André answered these questions (five; when he tried; never on purpose) but noticed that the interviewer had stopped making notes. When he commented on this, the interviewer apologized, refolded his legs, but in a different way, and pretended to write something on the sheet of paper in his clipboard.

André left the interview and met his mother, who was waiting outside. He was distressed. He held his ears in his hands until his mother made him stop. He was certain that he had failed the interview, that he should not have mentioned that he was autistic, that the interviewer struck him off at that point. His mother turned away, pressing the palms of her hands together, and grimaced. She was determined that she wasn't going to cry in front of him and remained sure that he didn't need to learn that his interviewers could guess that he was autistic, that the medical forms that she filled out on his behalf said so anyway, that they had to.

They were both surprised when, just two weeks later, he

received an acceptance letter, the first of many. His mother ran up and down the stairs in delight and relief. They were going to look past his time in an institution. It was OK that he had been slow to develop.

Craig had a similar experience with a college interviewer. He was being led around the college when, in the midst of a conversation, the subject of autism came up. The interviewer stopped and put her hand on his shoulder.

'But then you went to an ordinary school?' she checked.

'I went to a Jesuit school,' he replied.

She laughed. 'That's marvelous,' she remarked, and squeezed his shoulder before letting go. From that point on, the tone of the tour changed. She started introducing locations by saying things like, 'This is where your arts lectures will be held,' rather than, 'This is where our students attend arts lectures.' They had been en route to her study for the interview but instead she walked around campus with him for forty-five minutes and then returned him to the main reception. The acceptance letter duly arrived in the post.

André finished up with five college admissions and Craig with seven. They both had good test scores but both knew other people with similar test scores who didn't do nearly as well. When they told me about how autism helped them get into college, I thought back to the admissions tutor at the college that I attended. When I spoke to her during an open day, with a letter from my high school before her – I read it afterwards and it mentioned the diagnosis of autism prominently – almost her first question was about my age. I told her – I was fifteen – and she beamed at me. 'I'll do my very best,' she said and touched my cheek. 'You should smile more,' she added. I remembered, too, the math teacher at the first primary school that I attended after leaving New York. She always looked at me expectantly when she introduced a new topic, as if she thought that I ought to take over the lesson, or that I might burst into flames if she didn't explain every concept just right.

Neither Craig nor André nor I have magnificent IQs. None of us have ever completed a crossword puzzle, and we couldn't with any rapidity reel off, for example, the next five prime numbers following ninety-one. However, people have frequently expected us to perform such feats. During the time that Craig wasn't particularly enjoying his under-graduate degree, a lecturer called him aside after a class and told him that he really should make more of his talent. This lecturer had no evidence that Craig possessed any talent. He hadn't, at that stage, read any essays, or marked any exam papers – this was the first semester of Craig's freshman year – but he had heard from a colleague that Craig was autistic and had memorized long passages from a range of philosophy books and this lecturer wanted Craig to ask more questions in class, to set out arguments ordered into steps, to deliver some of the quotations that he knew; he was disappointed that his autistic student wasn't being autistic, as he saw it, in class.

André, Craig and I are obviously very fortunate. We are towards that end of the autism spectrum from which it is simpler to progress into education, attainment, and employ-ment. There are many other autistic people who have to strain under the constraints of a different preconception. It is difficult to sustain a complaint about being mistaken for having an extraordinary mind; André, Craig and I have benefited from other people's hopes about how intelligent we might be. But many more autistic people undergo the assumption that they are fools, or idiots.

Randall can be in that position. While I was there, he was teased by men who asked him to transport guns around town. Since I was there, he broke up with Mike. It was a surprise to Mike that, for example, if Randall phoned home during the day to check what time they were meeting for dinner and Mike explained later that he hadn't answered because he was out jogging, then Randall might see that Mike's jogging trainers were lying together in the same postures as the day before – the left shoe on its side, the tip of the right one perched on the skirting board – and might conclude that it was unlikely that, having been moved, the shoes would be returned to exactly the same positions. Mike didn't believe that Randall would notice that there were sometimes hairs that belonged to neither of them on the pillows in their bed. Of course, Mike knew that Randall spotted details and yet Mike didn't think that Randall would be examining these details actively, so much so that he had no readymade answers when Randall confronted him with these inklings of infidelity. He sourly denied all the evidence that Randall mentioned, said mean things, and so Randall walked out. He moved back in with his parents and sent a friend of his around to collect his belongings a week later. Mike thought that he was outsmarting Randall, even that deceiving Randall was straightforward, and he was shocked when he found out otherwise; but he was also dismally contrite, like a vandal who just broke the urn containing his grandmother's ashes. Randall had made up his mind, however, and his parents stopped opening the door to Mike after a little while.

Sheila told me about a time when she was in a shopping center with Elizabeth. They had split up, so that Sheila could look at books and Elizabeth at clothes for herself. When Sheila went to find Elizabeth, she observed a group of young girls who had attached themselves to her daughter. Elizabeth was a careful shopper. Whenever she liked a piece of clothing, she unfolded it and felt around all the seams; she checked the quality of the lining, estimated the thread-count – Sheila's mother made her own clothes and she had delivered long tutorials to both daughter and granddaughter. When Elizabeth was disappointed by a garment that she had initially liked, she groaned. The girls who were following her were mocking these groans. They were imitating her and laughing. Elizabeth was too timid to confront them, so she was trying to continue shopping, but she was distressed and so her groans were gradually becoming louder and more sustained. Some of the girls were yelling names at her too.

Sheila intervened undramatically. She went over to her daughter and asked her what she thought of the skirt that she was looking at. She didn't glare at the girls, didn't even acknowledge them, and they filtered away. When Elizabeth took a few items into the fitting rooms, Sheila found a nearby security guard and expelled her anger. He shrugged his shoulders and explained that kids always gave mentally handicapped people a hard time and that he'd have stepped in if they pushed her or anything like that. Sheila gasped at this and almost fell over. Then, determined not to buy anything from the store and not ever to return there, she went back to the fitting rooms and subtly convinced Elizabeth that each of the items that she tried on weren't quite right.

Alongside these assumptions of credulity and cretin-hood, there is also the idea that autistic children are doomed, that there is no prospect for improvement – this leads either to despair or to the belief that autism itself has to be celebrated. Ira often had parents come to her and suggest that, as their child wasn't going to get radically better, wasn't it better to lessen the load of classes? Wasn't this intensive activity just wearing them out? The view that autism has to be defended as a distinctive way of being originates, I think, from the same core belief: autistic people don't really get better. And so, instead of trying to measure up to societal norms, autistic people should be permitted to maintain their own.

Autistic people are in a different position to deaf people, though, to take the example of another medical minority. Despite advances in technology, deaf people may remain unable to hear or speak with the same eloquence as they are able to sign. However, they *are* able to sign, and sign language is a highly textured form of communication. Arguably, we should allow deaf people to continue using it and cochlear implants may be the inappropriate bright idea of non-deaf people to eradicate a defect that deaf people don't perceive as being one. However, unless autistic people receive the right treatment and make as many advances as they are able to, they simply cannot engage in satisfying ways. There may be something distinctive about autistic minds, but at least some of that autism has to be removed, or eased, before autistic people can communicate meaningfully, even with one another, and set their minds upon the world. While there's no autistic equivalent of sign language, some level of intervention is necessary, and it doesn't often fail.

Ira and Rebecca were teasing me when they told me that I wasn't autistic any more. But there was more to it: they also meant that I didn't display as many of the symptoms as when they last knew me, twenty years before, and that I no longer had all the same limitations. I got better, to say it that way. And so did all of my former classmates, including those who are not in this book. It's unusual for autistic individuals to become top-rank speech-writers or computer scientists, like Craig or André, but progress is legion. However, what is significant isn't simply that we're all less idiotic than before; it's also the means, that we became this way through exposure to the world that lay beyond the horizon of our own selves.

The term autism derives from the Greek *autos*, meaning self. What joins all of the preconceptions summarized in this epilogue, which have recurred throughout the stories of my former classmates, is that they derive from the same belief, that autistic people are themselves only, self-enclosed and sealed off from the world.

The notion perpetrated on André, Craig and me has been that our minds are singular, glowing, remarkable, and un-touched by others. We are expected to be inept in social settings or with other people's feelings. We are expected to be brilliant with figures, or computer programs, or abstract ideas. It took Craig a long time to find a job after the 2004 elections. Being a Democrat, the possibilities were limited in a renewed Republican Capitol; however, though employers accepted that his prose might be exceptional, they weren't convinced that he could do anything else. For similar reasons, Mike believed that Randall would remain unaware of what was happening in his own bed. The girls who followed Elizabeth around the clothes store thought that she didn't realize what sounds she was making and that she didn't realize they were following her and that she wasn't sensible enough to be hurt by their taunts. And then there is a view that autistic people can't be reached, or that they shouldn't be, that their self-enclosure is or ought to be permanent.

What I've found, in each case, has been something rather different. Craig does write brilliant prose, but he learnt how to do it; his abilities were not innate. He has spoken to a lot of speech-writers to learn his craft; he's read a lot of books on the subject. Before he starts writing for anyone, he reads pages and pages of what they have said in the past, waits until he can hear the client's voice in his head, until he has grasped its distinctive heft and resonance. He is good at what he does, not because he is an unfathomable autodidact, but because he took the trouble to learn and because he tirelessly engages with his clients' minds. Randall worked out what Mike was doing to him. It wasn't a pleasant realization but he will be more savvy in relationships in the future. As Ira and Rebecca believed, with the evidence base provided by their working lives, other people, including but not limited to professionals, do make a difference to autistic people. That difference isn't always positive – Randall worries that he will find it hard to trust any future partner, and isn't he already a difficult person to be in a relationship with? – but it can be, especially when guided by experience and professional know-how. Our autism eased, in each case, because of other people, our parents, friends, and our teachers, of course.

This realization sometimes expands inside me until I feel as if my organs are going to bruise one another. It marks a big change in how autism is typically thought about. I have spoken to Craig about it too. Craig and I have become good friends. We have this idea of buying a bus and fitting it out with beds and computers, a grill and a blender for making milkshakes. We want to start in New York and drive around the US picking up all our former classmates, including those who are not in this book, including the boy that I only heard briefly from a telephone booth at a location that he wasn't able to disclose before the beeps began and the line cut out. I don't know where we intend to finish up. It's an odd idea. The bus is a sort of autistic ark, but where do we want to go and why should we go there together? Why only us? It's an odd idea, because clearly we need to stay where we are, in the jobs that we work, with the people that we've cultivated and who care about us.

The Idiots don't need to be sent anywhere. We're in the right place.

A Note on the Author

Kamran Nazeer was born of itinerant Pakistani parents and has lived in New York, Jeddah, Islamabad and Glasgow. He studied law but decided not to become a lawyer. By the time he completed his PhD thesis, he had decided not to become an academic. On leaving Cambridge, he was recruited into Her Majesty's Service and now works as a policy adviser in Whitehall. His writing has been published in newspapers and magazines. *Send in the Idiots* is his first book.